Historical Association Studies

Secrecy in Britain

Historical Association Studies
General Editors: M. E. Chamberlain and James Shields

China in the Twentieth-Century
Paul Bailey

The French Reformation
Mark Greengrass

The Ancien Régime
Peter Campbell

Politics in the Reign of Charles II
K. H. D. Haley

Decolonization
The Fall of the European Empires
M. E. Chamberlain

Occupied France
Collaboration and Resistance
1940–1944
H. R. Kedward

Gandhi
Anthony Copley

Secrecy in Britain
Clive Ponting

The Counter-Reformation
N. S. Davidson

Appeasement
Keith Robbins

British Radicalism and the French
Revolution 1789–1815
H. T. Dickinson

Franklin D. Roosevelt
Michael Simpson

From Luddism to the First Reform Bill
Reform in England 1810–1832
J. R. Dinwiddy

Britain's Decline
Problems and Perspectives
Alan Sked

Radicalism in the English
Revolution 1640–1660
F. D. Dow

The Cold War 1945–1965
Joseph Smith

Bismarck
Bruce Waller

Revolution and Counter-Revolution
in France 1815–1852
William Fortescue

The Russian Revolution
1917–1921
Beryl Williams

The New Monarchy
England, 1471–1534
Anthony Goodman

The Historical Association, 59a Kennington Park Road, London SE11 4JH

Secrecy in Britain

CLIVE PONTING

Basil Blackwell

Copyright © Clive Ponting 1990

First published 1990

Basil Blackwell Ltd
108 Cowley Road, Oxford, OX4 1JF, UK

Basil Blackwell, Inc.
3 Cambridge Center
Cambridge, MA 02142, USA

British Library Cataloguing in Publication Data

A CIP catalogue record for this book is available
from the British Library.

Library of Congress Cataloging in Publication Data

Ponting, Clive.
    Secrecy in Britain/Clive Ponting.
       p.   cm. — (Historical Association studies)
    Bibliography: p.
    Includes index.
    ISBN 0−631−16912−1
    1. Official secrets — Great Britain. I. Title. II. Series.
JN329.S4P66   1989
323.44′5′0941−dc20   89−34768
                                         CIP

Typeset in 10 on 11 pt Ehrhardt
by Setrite
Printed in Great Britain by Whitstable Litho Ltd, Whitstable, Kent.

Contents

Abbreviations

BBC	British Broadcasting Corporation
CEGB	Central Electricity Generating Board
CID	Committee of Imperial Defence
CND	Campaign for Nuclear Disarmament
D-Notice	Defence Notice
EEC	European Economic Community
FOI	Freedom of Information
GC&CS	Government Code & Cypher School (later GCHQ)
GCHQ	Government Communications Headquarters
ITV	Independent Television
M15	Security Service (internal subversion)
M16	Secret Intelligence Service (overseas intelligence)
M19	Department of postal censors (initially MO9)
MO9	Department of postal censors (later MI9)
MoD	Ministry of Defence
MOT	Ministry of Transport
MP	Member of Parliament
OSA	Official Secrets Act
PCO	Passport Control Officers
PRO	Public Records Office
RAF	Royal Air Force
SSB	Secret Service Bureau
SIS	Secret Intelligence Service
UK	United Kingdom (of Great Britain and Northern Ireland)
UKAEA	United Kingdom Atomic Energy Authority

Chronology

1703	Decyphering Branch founded
1797	Secret Service Vote established
1833	Government granted injunction against sale of diplomatic papers
1844	Decyphering Branch abolished
1858	First use of criminal law (Larceny Act) for unauthorized disclosure
1873	Intelligence Branch (later Intelligence Department) established in War Office
1883	Formation of Foreign Intelligence Committee
1884	Start of the 'lobby system'
1886	Naval Intelligence Department established
	Special Branch established
1889	Official Secrets Act 1889 passed
1909–10	Secret Service Bureau formed (with military and naval intelligence departments; home department for counter-espionage (ancestor of MI5); and foreign department for espionage (forerunner of MI6))
1911	Official Secrets Act 1911 passed (repealed OSA 1889)
1912	D-Notice Committee established
1914	Room 40 (cryptography section) set up
1919	Government Code and Cypher School (later GCHQ) established.
	Secret Service Committee set up.
1920	Official Secrets Act 1920 passed (amended OSA 1911)
1924	Zinoviev Letter Affair
1933	Trial of Compton Mackenzie
1934	Trial of Edgar Lansbury
1937	Lewis Case (use of section 6 against a journalist)
1938	Duncan Sandys Affair (use of section 6 against an MP)
1939	Official Secrets Act 1939 passed (amended section 6 of OSA 1920)
1952	Maxwell-Fyfe directive on MI5 operations
1954	Grigg Report on Public Records
1957	Birkett Report on Interception of Communications
1958	Public Records Act 1958 (introduced the 'fifty-year rule')

1   The Secrecy Laws

The extent and nature of official secrecy is the missing ingredient from most historical discussion of modern Britain. The historian working from government archives can easily overlook how little of the information they contain was actually known to other people at the time. This is particularly the case if, as in Britain, the governing elite hold the view that the whole process of government must be kept confidential. In such circumstances many of the facts revealed in historical studies based on official material would not have been public knowledge. A comparison of historical research and contemporary media coverage will usually reveal that the press and public were seriously ignorant, misinformed or misled about the real assumptions, motives and actions of the government of the day.

Britain has one of the most extensive systems to control the flow of official information of any Western democracy. For the last century it has been a criminal offence to reveal official information without authority. Over 100 statutes prohibit disclosure of information of all kinds. Unofficial curbs and pressures reinforce the statutory provisions and curtail the freedom of the press. A powerful and persistent culture of secrecy − reflecting the basic assumption that good government is closed government and the public should only be allowed to know what the government decides they should know − was carried over from the nineteenth century and refined in the twentieth century when it was given statutory backing through Britain's formidable secrecy laws.

For most of the nineteenth century Britain had no laws to enforce secrecy. Control of official information was exercised through an informal code of conduct among the elite group of politicians and administrators, who had a strong common interest in treating the conduct of public affairs as an essentially private matter. This situation began to change in the late nineteenth century under two pressures − one internal to the government, the other external. As

1

the functions of government departments expanded and the number of civil servants increased, the process of government was less the preserve of an elite, and group loyalty declined. The number of newspapers and readers also grew. This created pressure for more information and the problem of how to keep information away from the general public and the press began to preoccupy Whitehall. The response of ministers and civil servants was to create a strong statutory framework that would enforce secrecy and replace the previously accepted common code of conduct among the elite.

Two main problem areas had already emerged during the early nineteenth century — control of historical papers and leaks to the press about current affairs. There were a number of cases where documents that diplomats and other government officials had acquired in the course of their work and retained as part of their personal papers were put up for sale. The government resorted to injunctions under the civil law, with varying success, in order to prevent the sale or publication of such documents on the grounds that they were the property of the State rather than the individual. In 1833 Lord Hanley's papers about Britain's foreign relations in the period 1777–89 were put up for auction. The government pressed ahead with obtaining an injunction, even though the papers were withdrawn from sale. Four years later the Foreign Office tried unsuccessfully to stop publication of dispatches sent from Spain by Lord Wellesley in 1809. In 1847 they also failed to establish ownership and prevent *The Times* publishing correspondence concerning the Congress of Vienna of 1815. In a variation on the theme Lady Jackson, widow of a British diplomat, tried in 1862 to sell some dispatches to the Foreign Office for £3,000. She was served with an injunction, but the Foreign Office ended up paying £800 for the return of the papers. In 1865 they returned to the civil courts for an injunction to prevent the possible sale of the Buckingham and Grenville papers relating to the Peace of Fontainebleau in 1762. (At the time no Foreign Office papers later than 1760 were available for public inspection).

In an attempt to deal with civil servants who leaked information to the press, the government decided to make use of the existing criminal law. The difficulty here was that in the absence of any legal protection of official information as such their case could only be based on property rights. As in the civil courts, the government argued that Crown servants had no right to physically remove or otherwise dispose of documents which came into their possession as a result of their employment. In two well-publicized cases the prosecution proved unable to make theft charges stick.

On 12 November 1858 the *Daily News* printed two confidential dispatches dating from June 1857 and June 1858. Sent by the Lord High Commissioner in the Ionian Islands to the Colonial Office, they dealt with the sensitive state of affairs in the islands, where the inhabitants were demanding union with Greece. The timing and contents of the leak were embarrassing for the government, as Gladstone was on his way to prepare a report on the situation and the dispatches appeared to prejudge the outcome of his mission. The leak was traced to William Guernsey, who, while visiting a friend employed in the Colonial Office library, had removed a copy of the documents and supplied them, without payment, to the newspaper. The prosecution was conducted by the Attorney-General in person, who told the court that it was impossible to overrate the serious consequences that might result from the publication of such important documents. There had already been serious complications with foreign governments. Guernsey's skilful defence persuaded the judge to direct the jury that the *Daily News* had acted quite properly in publishing the dispatches even though they were marked confidential, and he raised doubts as to whether there was sufficient evidence to sustain a charge of larceny. It took the jury fifteen minutes to acquit Guernsey.

Another prosecution was brought in 1878, this time under the Larceny Act of 1861. It followed publication in a special late night edition of the *Globe* on 30 May of details of a secret agreement between Russia and Britain on the eve of the Congress of Berlin, where the major powers were poised to tackle the Eastern Question. Earlier that day Charles Marvin, a poorly paid temporary clerk in the treaty department of the Foreign Office, had been asked to copy out the text of the agreement between Lord Salisbury and the Russian ambassador. Marvin, who supplemented his income of £90 a year through occasional contributions to the *Globe*, passed on the details to the newspaper in return for a payment of forty guineas. Challenged in the House of Lords, Salisbury dismissed the press report as wholly unauthentic. This denial was to lead to still greater diplomatic embarrassment for the British government. An outraged Marvin sent a private and confidential letter in his own name to several editors to assert the accuracy of the story and he also copied out the text and sent it to the *Globe*, which published the first eleven clauses of the secret agreement (which confirmed that Salisbury had deliberately misled the House of Lords) on the front page on 14 June, the day after the start of the Congress.

After the editor of the *Morning Advertiser* informed the police about the letter, Marvin was arrested and charged with removing a document and stealing the paper on which he had passed the information to the newspaper.

At the hearing before Bow Street magistrates it turned out that Marvin had copied the contents of the government document onto his own paper. The prosecution case was further undermined when the head of the treaty department had to admit under cross-examination that there was no rule which forbade Foreign Office clerks writing to the newspapers. The chief magistrate accepted Marvin's evidence that he had been given good reason to believe the information would be circulated among the press the next morning. He concluded there was insufficient evidence of larceny and dismissed the summons. Marvin lost his job but went on to become a minor celebrity and successful author, later dedicating his memoirs in gratitude to the editor of the *Morning Advertiser*.

One immediate result of the Marvin affair was the introduction of new rules. From the early 1870s there were piecemeal changes to the code of conduct for civil servants in order to try to stop leaks. In 1873, under the heading 'Premature Disclosure of Official Documents', the Treasury issued a minute which roundly condemned leaks to the press as

> offences of the gravest character to which most civil servants would not stoop. The unauthorised use of official information is the worst fault a civil servant can commit. It is on the same footing as cowardice by a soldier. It is unprofessional. (Hooper, 1987, p. 21)

The threat of dismissal was made, but the Treasury hoped that the service would itself want to check 'a practice which injured its reputation for fidelity and honour'. A further minute issued in 1875 reminded any employees with press connections of the penalty for breach of trust, but not until after the Marvin case three years later were such links expressly prohibited. The leaks continued, and in 1884, after an incident when news about General Gordon became public before it was announced in Parliament, the Treasury decided to spell out the requirement for absolute confidentiality. A further minute stated that the publication, without authority, of official information was grounds for dismissal, with no distinctions to be drawn between the degree of harm involved. The need for secrecy, it pointed out, was 'not confined to matters still under discussion, but included also the unauthorised disclosure of matters finally decided upon' (Hooper, 1987, p. 21).

Inside the Civil Service the rules had thus been gradually clarified and progressively tightened. They have remained in force to this day: all official information, regardless of content or classification, is to be regarded as confidential unless it is decided otherwise. There must be no unauthorized disclosure of information. But neither these early instructions nor later versions laid down a general procedure to be followed in granting or obtaining 'authorization'.

An episode in 1887 served to highlight the deficiency in the law even more acutely than the Guernsey and Marvin cases had done. A draughtsman named Terry Young was found to be responsible for the sale of warship designs, probably to the French. He was dismissed but it was felt there was not enough evidence to prosecute him. The First Lord of the Admiralty told Parliament that a criminal law which allowed someone like Terry to escape could not be regarded as satisfactory, and that consideration was being given to strengthening the law.

Work began on drafting new legislation in 1887. The task was undertaken initially by the Admiralty, but then taken over by the Treasury. The first draft did not include espionage but this was added at the request of the Foreign Office. What emerged in 1888 was originally called the Breach of Official Trust Bill. It was afterwards amended, renamed and re-presented to become the Official Secrets Act (OSA) of 1889. The government responsible for introducing Britain's first secrecy law was led by Lord Salisbury, who had become Prime Minister in 1886. (As Foreign Secretary he had suffered serious political and diplomatic embarrassment arising out of the Marvin case.) The original title of the draft bill reflected its primary purpose: the intention was to cover not just espionage but all cases where officials disclosed information without authority regardless of the damage done. The all-embracing nature of secrecy legislation was apparent from the start.

The Act had a generally smooth passage: there was remarkably little debate in either House, and none at all about the wide scope of the new law. The Lord Chancellor, Lord Halsbury, recalled that there had been in recent years conspicuous examples of the need to guard official secrets, and protect official documents. He put the emphasis on patriotism and espionage, and mentioned the prohibition of any disclosure of any official information almost as an afterthought:

It is a duty which every citizen owes to his country, that he should not facilitate the military operations of other countries by giving copies of official documents, and the Bill is intended to remedy existing defects in our law in that respect. It provides for the punishment of those persons who either give information to the enemies of the country, or who act as spies, or make or communicate plans or sketches of fortresses and like places, or disclose official secrets. (Hansard, 11 July 1889)

In the House of Commons the bill was introduced by a speech from the Attorney-General, Sir Richard Webster, remarkable chiefly for its brevity:

Sir, I wish to say just a word or two with regard to this Bill. It has been prepared under the direction of the Secretary of State for War and the First Lord of the Admiralty in order to punish the offence of obtaining information and communicating it against the interests of the state. The Bill is an exceedingly simple one and I beg to move its second reading. (Hansard, 28 March 1889)

Again debate was limited and largely confined to mention of treason and espionage. However one MP successfully took up the issue of how the wording of one section might operate against the public interest. The Attorney-General conceded that if the reference to disclosure 'contrary to the interests of any part of the government' were retained in the bill, it could make criticism of a government department — which could be for the benefit of the state in many instances — into a crime. Under the provisions eventually adopted, an offence was committed if information had been communicated to a person to whom it ought not to have been *and* the communication was not in the interests of the State.

The Act remained in force for just over twenty years, and was seldom used. Leaks continued despite the introduction of criminal sanctions to reinforce the penalties already available under Civil Service discipline. The only prosecution brought under the 1889 OSA without genuine security implications was the case of John Doe. He was a clerk in the supply depot at Woolwich Dockyard, who wrote to a contractor offering to supply details of prices charged by their competitors. The court heard that Doe had not been told that these documents were confidential, and that there was no copy of the OSA in his office. He was found guilty, but the jury said they did not think Doe knew he was committing a criminal offence. The judge merely bound him over to come up for judgment if called upon to do so.

The government began to consider stiffening the 1889 Act within a decade of its passage. Further press stories based on leaks served to highlight the fact that the existing law did not make either receipt or publication of unauthorized disclosures a criminal offence, so no steps could be taken against the newspapers themselves. From the turn of the century fears of a German invasion and highly coloured stories of German spies infiltrating Britain began to proliferate. Foreign espionage now seemed a threat to be countered.

There were two abortive attempts at introducing new legislation during this period. The first came in 1896 when a draft bill was introduced which would have placed the burden of proof on the accused, to show he had obtained official information for innocent purposes and not for the use of a foreign government. The proposals were again outlined very briefly by the Attorney-General, Sir Richard Webster, who said that cases had arisen where convictions had failed due to the impossibility of obtaining evidence. After an opposition MP objected to the way that the Attorney-General had made light of shifting the burden of proof from the prosecution the debate was adjourned and the bill was subsequently withdrawn. In March 1908 another bill which would have introduced fundamental changes to the law was presented to Parliament by the Liberal Government of Campbell-Bannerman. (In Britain party politics played little, if any, role in the development of strong state control over information. Indeed it was the same Liberal Government (under Asquith) that established the full framework of 'national security' – the Official Secrets Act of 1911, informal censorship of the press and the forerunners of both MI5 and MI6 – all within a period of a few years.) As well as strengthening the espionage provisions the new bill would have prohibited the unauthorized *publication* of official information, if publication was not in the interests of the State. It also proposed to extend criminal sanctions to cover any member of the public, not just Crown servants and government contractors. On this occasion the proposals met with such serious opposition both in Parliament and in the press that the bill was withdrawn. It was seen as a threat to free speech and an abuse of the government's powers. Lord Loreburn,

7

the Lord Chancellor, did admit there were great difficulties in reconciling freedom of publication with the need to protect secret documents and information in the public interest. However, he assured his fellow peers that anyone in the press conducting his duties honourably would be quite safe. In May the Lord Chancellor announced the second reading was being postponed because of representations made by the press that it would interfere with their legitimate enterprise and freedom, although he assured them that His Majesty's Government had no such designs.

The background to the introduction of the Official Secrets Act of 1911 is often described as being the German spy scare (which by 1909 had created a mood bordering on public hysteria) and the Agadir Crisis (when fears of a European war followed the appearance of the German gunboat *Panther* off Morocco). This is only true in the sense that these episodes created the immediate context in which a new bill was passed. Certainly it is an interpretation of events which reflects the impression of national emergency deliberately conveyed by Asquith's Government. The real origins of the 1911 Act lie in the longstanding desire on the part of successive governments for control over official information, for effective sanctions to deter civil servants from disclosing any information without authority, and for a means of mounting successful prosecutions in the event of a leak. The advantages of linking protection against disclosure generally with the aim of protection against espionage had been evident since the relatively trouble-free passage of the first secrecy law in 1889. The experience of 1908 demonstrated that attempts to widen the law might well run into serious trouble unless carefully presented.

In March 1909, at the request of the military, Asquith set up a special sub-committee of the Committee of Imperial Defence (CID) to assess the foreign espionage threat and consider the need for extra powers in times of emergency to deal with persons suspected of being spies or secret service agents. A paper submitted by the Home Office on the 1889 OSA suggested amendments confined to espionage. The Secretary to the Committee noted that an amending bill on these lines 'need contain no reference to the publication of documents or information . . . it would therefore not be of so controversial a nature or excite such opposition as would be caused by any clause which might be suspect of interfering with the liberties of the press' (Ponting, 1985, p. 18). This approach, however, was to change radically following an intervention from the First Lord of the Admiralty, Reginald McKenna, at the third meeting of the committee on 12 July:

> Mr McKenna pointed out that the *Daily Mail* had recently
> published details regarding one of our battleships which the
> Admiralty desired to keep secret. We ought to be in a
> position to prosecute the proprietor of the paper for doing
> this. We are, however, quite powerless in the matter, as the
> Official Secrets Act does not provide us with any machinery
> for instituting such a prosecution. (Ponting, 1985, p. 18)

The Committee's report was presented on 24 July. It was considered so sensitive that only one copy of the proposals was made. As well as recommending the establishment of a Secret Service bureau, they endorsed the need for a measure to reinforce existing espionage provisions and suggested in addition a separate bill, to be produced after negotiation with the press, to cover McKenna's proposals for tight control over government information and specific powers against the press. Recognizing the controversial nature of this proposal, they argued:

> such a Bill would excite less opposition if it were introduced
> by the Secretary of State for War than by the Home Office,
> and that this might be done on the plea of its being a
> measure of precaution of great importance to the national
> defence. (Ponting, 1985, p. 19)

Work went ahead, drawing heavily on the draft bills of 1896 and 1908, and a new bill was ready by 1910. The way that the passage of this bill was engineered reveals that the committee's idea of a diversionary ploy had been adopted. There is, however, no evidence of any discussions with the press, and the government obviously opted for the additional protective cover of continuing to combine espionage and disclosure of any official information in the same act.

In the summer of 1911 the government decided the time was right to bring in its new bill. On 17 July it was introduced into the House of Lords and given a second reading on 25 July. Lord Haldane, Secretary of State for War, mendaciously explained the purpose was not to enact new restrictions but to make the existing law more effective. There was nothing new about the act, it was merely a change in procedure. Only three other peers spoke in the debate; following Haldane's lead they too were concerned about strengthening the law against espionage and protecting defence secrets. The bill was passed without amendment and came to the House of Commons on 18 August. The Under-Secretary of State for War, Colonel J. E. B. Seely, told the House it was 'undoubtedly in the public interest that this Bill should be passed, and passed at once' (Hansard, 18 August 1911). In an extremely short speech to propose the second reading he offered a few words of sweeping reassurance to justify the unprecedented speed and lack of time for debate:

> The actual change in the law is slight, and it is perfectly true to say that none of His Majesty's loyal subjects run the least risk whatever of having their liberties infringed in any degree or particular whatever. (Hansard, 18 August 1911)

The government's tactics were to create an atmosphere of urgency and avoid any real debate. Colonel Seely's account of proceedings gives the impression of a bold gamble brilliantly pulled off. He recalled the mounting tension after he rose to move the bill in committee:

> This was the first critical moment; two men got up to speak, but both were forcibly pulled down by their neighbours after they had uttered a few sentences, and the committee stage was passed. The Speaker walked back to his chair and said: 'The question is, that I report this Bill without amendment to the House.' Again two or three people stood up; again they were pulled down by their neighbours, and the report stage was through. The Speaker turned to me and said: 'The third reading, what day?' 'Now, Sir,' I replied. My heart beat fast as the Speaker said: 'The question is that this Bill be read a third time.' It was open to any one of all the members of the House of Commons to get up and say that no Bill had ever yet passed through all its stages in one day without a word of explanation from the Minister in charge... But to the eternal honour of those members ... not one man seriously opposed. (Hooper, 1987, p. 30)

It took about forty minutes for the bill to go through all its stages. There was no discussion of section 2. There was a brief protest about the wording of section 1, and one MP did complain it was an extraordinary thing to pass such a bill without an opportunity of discussing it and felt it upset Magna Charta, but he went on to vote for it. In his soothing and misleading intervention the Attorney-General went still further than Seely in playing down the significance of the proposals: 'Of course, this House knows that the principle of the Bill is not new ... There is nothing novel in the principle of the Bill' (Hansard, 18 August 1911).

The presentation, speed and timing all combined to ensure an unimpeded passage for the new Official Secrets Act. Far from being hastily drafted provisions introduced in response to an emergency, the new measures were the product of a prolonged period of preparation in Whitehall. The 1889 Act was seen as being too weak: it had to be repealed and replaced with a stronger and more wide-ranging law. A decision was taken secretly in 1909 to present the new criminal offences enshrined in section 2 as an integral part of national security and was successfully executed in 1911. Colonel Seely himself later described it as a formidable piece of legislation. The real extent of Britain's secrecy laws did not become apparent to Parliament, the press and the public until much later.

Section 1 of the Act dealt with espionage offences, and the main change here was to shift the burden of proof: it was no longer for the prosecution to prove guilt, it was for the defence to prove innocence. It was this change that in effect provided parliamentary cover for the introduction of section 2. This created two main offences: unauthorized communication and unauthorized receipt of official information. The text itself is unwieldy and obscure in places, but the basic intention was unmistakable: every piece of government information was covered. It became an offence, punishable by up to two year's imprisonment and an unlimited fine, for a Crown servant to communicate such information 'to any person, other than a person to whom he is authorised to communicate it, or a person to whom it is in the interest of the State his duty to communicate it' (Official Secrets Act 1911, section 2). Anyone receiving information, knowing or having reasonable grounds to believe that it had been communicated in contravention of the Act, also committed an offence unless he could prove the communication was contrary to his desire. So the scope of the law was widened considerably; whereas the 1889 Act had introduced criminal penalties for civil servants and government contractors, by making receipt an offence, the 1911 Act extended the threat of criminal sanctions to cover the press and the general public.

The marked absence of contemporary public scrutiny of section 2 was followed by a good deal of public debate and critical examination of its strengths and weaknesses as a vehicle for maintaining official secrecy. It was the subject of a government inquiry

11

by the Franks Committee, which published a report in 1972 containing major criticisms, above all of its enormously wide scope:

> The leading characteristic [is] its catch-all quality. It catches all official documents and information. It makes no distinction of kind, and no distinction of degree. All information which a Crown servant learns in the course of his duty is 'official' for the purposes of section two, whatever its nature, whatever its importance, whatever its original source. A blanket is thrown over everything: nothing escapes. (Cmnd 5104, par. 17)

This meant that there were innumerable technical contraventions of the Act every day: every time, for instance, a civil servant went home and mentioned any aspect of his work, however trivial, to the 'unauthorized' members of his family. The old joke about the menu in the civil service canteen being an official secret may sound absurd but it was nonetheless true within the meaning of the Act. There was an early test case about its intended scope. Albert Crisp, a War Office statistics clerk, was charged with communicating details of clothing contracts and his friend, Arthur Homewood, a director of a tailoring firm, was charged with receipt. At Westminster police court the magistrate took the view that something called the Official Secrets Act was intended to apply to matters that were secret, and there was nothing secret about clothing contracts; he could see no public interest in keeping details of executed contracts secret and acquitted the defendants. To get round this set-back, the Attorney-General preferred an indictment against Crisp and Homewood and obtained a high court ruling that section 2 applied to any official document or information obtained as a result of employment by the Crown.

A further much criticized feature of section 2 was its lack of clarity. Franks described it as 'a mess'. It has been calculated that its various sub-sections could produce a total of 2,314 possible offences. There was no attempt to define 'official secret', 'authorization', 'duty' or 'interest of the State'. As a result of ambiguous wording judges failed to agree as to whether *mens rea* (the criterion of a guilty mind) applied. According to Mr Justice Caulfield in the Aitken Case (p. 61), to be guilty a person had to know or believe he was communicating information in breach of the OSA, whereas Mr Justice McCowan in the Ponting Case (p. 64) took the view it was an absolute offence, and the prosecution had only to show the

12

information had been communicated without authority. Similar legal confusion surrounded the question of whether the wording did allow a 'public interest defence'. Ponting's defence against the charge of unauthorized communication was based on 'duty in the interest of the State', but the judge ruled that the interest of the State was identical to the interests of the government of the day.

Another feature, sometimes held up as a redeeming one designed to prevent merely frivolous or otherwise inappropriate use of section 2, was the need for the Attorney-General's consent to any prosecution. However, this supposed safeguard itself gave rise to controversy. Arguably it undermined what should be a basic principle of the rule of law, namely the degree of certainty about what acts will be punished. Moreover the fact that the decision whether or not to prosecute was made by a man with the dual role of law officer and government Minister inevitably gave rise to doubts as to his neutrality and concerns about political pressures influencing the decision. The judge in the Aitken Trial said he thought the act could be viciously or capriciously used by a embarrassed government. The concern about political abuse also emerged in the Franks Report:

A number of witnesses pointed out that Section 2 could be used to serve the political interests of a Government, or to save Ministers or officials from embarrassment. (Cmnd 5104, par. 41)

However formidable the new secrecy legislation that was passed so rapidly in 1911, there were renewed pressures in the wake of the First World War for a further strengthening of the law. During the war stringent Defence of the Realm regulations had been in force, and when these lapsed the government, loathe to lose the extra powers, set up a review of peacetime requirements. The government finally decided on a series of wide-ranging amendments to the existing Act, which were eventually adopted in the form of the Official Secrets Act 1920. It introduced an array of new offences. For example, activities such as unlawfully wearing a military uniform, making a false statement or possessing an official stamp if committed (in the very widely drawn words of the new Act) 'for any purpose prejudicial to the safety or interest of the State' were made punishable by up to two years' imprisonment, with or without hard labour. A new section 6 made it an offence to fail to give information as to the commission of any offence under the Official Secrets Acts. This made it impossible for a suspect to remain silent under police questioning and it was later used in a highly controversial way against the press and an MP (see p. 60). A new section 7 made it an offence to commit any act preparatory to an offence under the OSA.

The new bill was introduced in the House of Lords in June 1920. Once again there was a troubled background with growing concern about Bolshevik subversion and the threat of civil war in Ireland. This time the government's proposals did not have quite such a smooth passage. But it was not until the third reading that some of their Lordships ventured to express disquiet. Viscount Burnham, although 'loath to interrupt the silent course of proceedings', thought some of the wording dangerously wide, and was concerned about what might happen to editors who came into possession of embarrassing official documents. Lord Parmoor regretted such a bill was necessary 'because it will seriously interfere with our ordinary freedom in various directions'. As Viscount Peel for the government was taken unawares, he suggested that the question of amendments be deferred to the House of Commons (Hooper 1987, pp. 34–5). The second reading there took place only days after 'Bloody Sunday' when twelve British intelligence officers were killed in Dublin. The government's tactics were to concentrate on the need for strengthening and updating the law against spies, backed up by reference to experience gained during the war. The Attorney-General, Sir Gordon Hewart, played down the significance of the new powers being sought, describing them as 'certain ancillary provisions, the better to secure the end already sought to be secured' (Hansard, 2 December 1920). Although at the outset he had acknowledged he could not possibly say the bill dealt only with spying, he went on to give a number of deliberately misleading reassurances about specific provisions when these came under challenge in the debate. Asked specifically about powers of police questioning under section 6, he retorted quite incorrectly: 'We are dealing only with offences or suspected offences under the principal Act, or this Act, in other words, to put it shortly, we are dealing with spying or attempts at spying'. He found the suggestion that the bill dealt with the press 'an astonishing statement' (Hansard, 2 December 1920).

The most outspoken opposition to the bill came from Sir Donald Maclean, a Liberal MP, who believed the Act would impinge on the legitimate functions of the press and the liberty of the individual. He objected to the reversal of the burden of proof as 'the complete abrogation of any semblance of justice' and to a measure which could involve prosecuting a newspaper editor in the same way as an enemy spy in time of war. He was particulary incensed by the powers under section 6 and section 8 (providing for secret hearings):

> I find it difficult to confine my language in regard to this Bill within the range of parliamentary propriety. It is another attempt to clamp the powers of war on to the liberties of the citizen in peace. (Hansard, 2 December 1920)

Despite this opposition and more criticism in the press, the Act was passed, without any significant changes and with little detailed scrutiny of its provisions. Apart from introducing a whole series of new criminal sanctions previously only thought necessary in time of war, the distinction between espionage offences and breaches of official trust had been further blurred by the introduction of provisions which applied equally to both. With the introduction of this new Act, the legal framework for secrecy was in place.

2   Growth of the Secret State

Early this century the British Government began to develop an extensive secret intelligence network. The three main organizations are still operating today. The Security Service or MI5 deals with internal subversion, the Secret Intelligence Service or MI6 gathers overseas intelligence and the Government Communications Headquarters or GCHQ is responsible for the interception of communications and codebreaking. For much of the time since they were established there has been no official recognition that they even exist. Their size, cost and activities remain closely guarded secrets. They are entirely under executive control; there is no parliamentary oversight. Official records relating to their work are withheld almost entirely from public disclosure indefinitely.

Current or recent operations of all secret services and intelligence agencies are naturally surrounded by secrecy, but in Britain a policy of maintaining total secrecy about virtually every aspect of their work was adopted at an early stage, and is still taken to extraordinary lengths today. There is no system for formally vetting the memoirs of former agents, as happens with their US counterparts. Information about their historical development has had to be collected in piecemeal fashion and patched together from a variety of sources, including errors and omissions in the official 'weeding' of documents released to the Public Record Office and the trickle of memoirs by former agents who were sufficiently obstinate or privileged enough to get their stories into print despite the official ban. The resulting picture is inevitably patchy, but without an account of the growth of the secret state, both the history of the period and the history of official secrecy are incomplete. The experience of other Western democracies demonstrates that a doctrine of total secrecy is neither inevitable nor indispensable for the successful operation of intelligence agencies in peacetime. In Britain, however, absolute secrecy has been the policy of all post-war governments, conditioned by two principles: that intelligence cannot be discussed in public, and that Parliament has to surrender all its powers in intelligence matters to the executive.

The early history of secret intelligence activity is characterized chiefly by informality and the intermittent interest of government. There were periods when the use of spies and informers on a casual basis was encouraged, as at the time of the French Revolution or during bouts of Chartist or Fenian agitation. Occasionally a more organized network of agents might be established as by Sir Francis Walsingham for Elizabeth I or John Thurloe for Oliver Cromwell. From the Restoration there was a Secret Service Fund, but this was used, or abused, for multifarious secret purposes including political bribes and royal mistresses. From 1797 on there has been an annual Secret Service Vote, but this too provided a convenient source of miscellaneous expenditure until tighter controls were gradually imposed. During the nineteenth century much of the money went on freelance amateurs engaged by the Foreign Office, and the level of expenditure fluctuated a good deal. It reached over £172,000 in 1805 then fell off to a level of about £40,000 towards the end of the century. Although the late Victorian Foreign Office was putting its administrative and diplomatic effort on a more professional basis, this process of reform did not extend to its secret intelligence system.

Before the 1870s the nearest thing to a professional organization was probably the tiny Decyphering Branch founded in 1703, but even this was a part-time activity undertaken by a few country gentlemen and clerics. It was abolished altogether in 1844 following a parliamentary row over disclosures about opening the correspondence of the exiled Italian nationalist leader, Mazzini. The first steps towards a permanent intelligence organization were taken in the War Office amid the debacle of the Crimean War with the setting up of the Topographical and Statistical Department in 1855. The War Office first stated a formal requirement to collect information on foreign armies in 1871 and two years later established an Intelligence Branch. The Admiralty's approach remained even more low-key and haphazard until external pressures led to the formation of a Foreign Intelligence Committee in 1883 then a Naval Intelligence Department in 1886. During the 1880s there were also pressures to develop a more organized response to the Fenian threat, especially in the wake of the Phoenix Park murders in 1882. In 1886 a new body was set up to take on responsibility for dealing with all political crime, the Special Branch of the Metropolitan Police.

17

Despite the creation of new sections, secret intelligence activity remained mistrusted and neglected in military circles, although there were a few enthusiasts like Baden-Powell, who went on foreign trips disguised as a butterfly collector and regarded spying as sport. Even the chastening experiences of the Boer War only led to a temporary expansion of field intelligence and other 'special duties'. It was not considered necessary to retain in peacetime the new section set up at the start of the war to undertake censorship, counter-intelligence and 'secret service' duties. Perceptions began to change with the spread of scare stories about German spies and German invasion plans. A ready market for bogus intelligence and sightings of suspicious-looking aliens developed. When the *Daily Mail* serialized a book by William Le Queux called *The Invasion of 1910*, over a million copies were sold. Alarming reports circulated about waves of German reservists infiltrated into Britain variously disguised as waiters, cyclists and hairdressers and all bent on espionage. In March 1909 a sub-committee of the Committee of Imperial Defence was set up to consider the nature and extent of the foreign espionage threat. There was a marked lack both of hard information on Germany and of secret agents to obtain it, and the committee had to depend entirely on casual information. In retrospect the anecdotal evidence provided by the head of the War Office 'Special Section' appears remarkably flimsy and dubious, but in the end the committee concluded there was an extensive system of German espionage in Britain and no organiz-ation for countering it. It is now known that Germany did not have a spy network operating in Britain before the war; its efforts were concentrated on France and Russia.

As a result of the committee's report, produced later in 1909, the Secret Service Bureau (SSB) was established. Within a year it had not only military and naval sections but also a home department responsible for counter-espionage (the ancestor of MI5) and a foreign department in charge of espionage (the forerunner of MI6 or the Secret Intelligence Service). A lack of funds, personnel and professionalism prevented the SSB from achieving much before the war, although when Churchill became Home Secretary he helped to expand the role of the home department and its links with the police, for example by approving a secret register of aliens from likely enemy powers. The pressures brought on by the 1914–18 war led to internal re-organization and considerable expansion of the SSB. MI5 acquired its modern name in a War Office re-organization of January 1916 and by the armistice its original wartime staff of 19 had grown to 844. It had also enormously expanded its pre-war register of aliens to include British subjects and other nationals. By the spring of 1917 MI5's central registry contained 250,000 cards and 27,000 personal files, classified according to an elaborate scale ranging from AA (Absolutely Anglicized/ Allied) through to BB (Bad Boche). The most important wartime source of intelligence was probably cable and postal censorship. Despite some initial resistance from the Home and Foreign Offices to mass censorship of civilian mail, a department of postal censors (MO9 later MI9) was established in the War Office and by 1918 it was employing 4,800 censors.

After the First World War there was no return to the relatively small-scale pre-war agencies. The threat of subversion from the left led to the establishment of permanent, modern intelligence agencies. The post-war organization of the greatly expanded intelligence services was considered in a Secret Service Committee set up in 1919 under Lord Curzon, which met intermittently over the next two years. Its proposal for a 'civil secret service' to monitor subversion was approved and in May 1919 Sir Basil Thomson, then head of Special Branch, was also made head of a new Directorate of Intelligence under the Home Office, responsible for providing weekly reports for the Cabinet on subversion. In the aftermath of victory ministers were mainly concerned about domestic subversion, industrial unrest and Bolshevism. MI5 retained control of counter-espionage, but its budget was cut back sharply from its wartime level. Early in 1919 the Cabinet adopted another of Curzon's recommendations to establish a peacetime cryptographic unit. When the new Government Code and Cypher School (GC&CS) was set up, its publicly announced function was 'to advise as to the security of codes and cyphers used by all Government departments and to assist in their provision'. But its secret directive was 'to study the methods of cypher communications used by foreign powers' (Andrew, 1985, p. 232). After a break of some seventy years, the British Government had resumed interception of other governments' communications at the onset of the First World War and it has continued to do so ever since. However, for the first twenty years the new and highly secret organization was run on a shoe-string with fewer than sixty staff. In 1922 the Foreign Office took over direct responsibility from the Admiralty.

During the war MI5 had established a Military Control network which provided the basis of a counter-subversion system outside Britain. In 1919 this was transformed into a peacetime passport control system under the Foreign Office, with Passport Control Officers (PCO) attached to embassies and legations. Its role as originally conceived was to exclude Bolshevik agents from Britain and gather intelligence on Bolshevik subversion. This PCO network also came to provide foreign cover for the station chiefs of the Secret Intelligence Service or SIS. After a series of embarrassing incidents Thomson was dismissed and the Directorate of Intelligence disappeared with him, leaving Special Branch entirely under Scotland Yard and giving the SIS a much sought after monopoly of espionage and counter-intelligence work outside the UK and the British Empire. MI5's efforts were now concentrated on the domestic threat. What had started life as a Defence Black List with some 13,000 names became the 'Precautionary Index' and by 1925 it contained the names of over 25,000 people, in twelve categories, assessed as potentially dangerous to national security.

The high level of secrecy that surrounded all these activities posed particular problems with the arrival in 1923 of Ramsay MacDonald, Britain's first Labour Prime Minister, at the head of a minority government. Its members were unaware of the code-breaking duties of GC&CS and some of its leading lights had themselves been under surveillance. The various agencies maintained a policy of general reticence, but after experiencing a wave of labour unrest the government itself soon came to appreciate the role of domestic intelligence gathering. However, it seems clear from subsequent events that elements in the intelligence community did not reciprocate such feelings. The publication of the 'Zinoviev letter' in the *Daily Mail* just before the general election held in October 1924 caused a political sensation and almost certainly helped to ensure the Labour Government was not re-elected. The evidence points to the involvement of a former Director of Naval Intelligence, the connivance of Conservative Central Office and the help of serving officers in getting access to the document, although the identity and precise role of those involved have never been established with certainty. The letter (which the Soviet Union denounced as a forgery) dealt with Comintern policy abroad and its appearance in the press in fact pre-empted a decision by Ramsay MacDonald on whether to publish several similar documents in order to back up a challenge to the Soviet Government about their policy of supporting subversion in Britain. Its unofficial publication served instead to back up charges that the Labour Government was soft on Bolshevism, and to restore a Conservative Government to power. Internally the episode led to the circulation of secret intelligence material being severely curtailed.

From the start bitter rivalry and internecine conflict had characterized relations between the various parts of the intelligence community, and in 1931 there came another change in responsibilities. MI5 had long been arguing about the absurdity of dividing responsibility for monitoring civil and military subversion. Although it is now clear that the closely guarded secret of the Invergordon mutiny among ships of the Atlantic Fleet in September 1931 was in fact a spontaneous protest against wage cuts, at the time the incident was interpreted as further evidence of the dangers of subversion. Later that month responsibility for all investigations dealing with Communist and other foreign revolutionary movements was discreetly transferred from Scotland Yard to MI5, which increasingly described itself as the Security Service. Special Branch continued to make enquiries and arrests on its behalf and to provide camouflage for MI5 activities. From the 1930s the Security Service began to take an active interest in the threat of right-wing as well as left-wing subversion, and growing fears of German re-armament led to renewed government interest in the intelligence services generally. Decisions to increase spending were taken, although the question of the intelligence budget featured only once on the Cabinet agenda between 1936−9 and not at all in parliamentary discussion. The size of the Secret Service Vote rose from £180,000 in 1935 to £500,000 by 1939, but this was not enough to meet the growing costs. The Foreign Office and the Treasury were, therefore, asked to find some other means of provision, and ways were found of secretly diverting funds and concealing the sums within other departmental budgets (a practice which has continued ever since). On the operational front, probably the most sensitive aspect of interwar activity was MI5's attempts during the 1930s to open foreign diplomatic bags with the help of a secret department of the Post Office.

The fortunes of the intelligence services were transformed after Winston Churchill became Prime Minister in May 1940. His great belief in and enthusiasm for secret intelligence (especially code-breaking in the wake of increasing British access to the German 'Enigma' system from May 1940 on), helped to bring about a huge wartime expansion and modernization, and a Security Executive was set up at the end of May 1940 in the wake of the collapse of France to control work on internal security. The end of the war was again followed by a rundown and limited re-organization, although a number of wartime successes and the onset of the Cold

21

War ensured the process was less severe than after 1918. (Notable successes had included the 'Enigma' breakthrough and the double-cross system — where MI5 turned all German agents in the UK, but these were not revealed until the early 1970s.) The cryptographic effort, re-named Government Communication Headquarters (GCHQ) in 1942, moved to a new permanent site at Cheltenham and its priorities were switched to Soviet communications. The SIS (whose wartime recruits included Kim Philby) emerged without the major overhaul it needed. MI5 suffered much reduced resources and after 1945 an uneasy relationship with the new Labour Government, although what the Cabinet minutes called 'Communist endeavours to cause industrial unrest' helped to overcome ministerial suspicions. Without doubt the major legacy of the Second World War to the post-war history of British intelligence was the continuation of close Anglo-American co-operation. A secret wartime agreement to share signals intelligence with the Americans formed the basis of the secret agreement, whose existence is still not acknowledged, signed in 1947. It provides for co-operation in the intelligence field between the UK and the United States and to a lesser extent with Canada, Australia and New Zealand.

The post-war history of the secret and intelligence services offers no evidence of any voluntary slackening of the policy of absolute secrecy on the part of successive governments. The classic formulation of the prevailing doctrine is ascribed to Austen Chamberlain when he addressed the House of Commons as Foreign Secretary in November 1924:

It is of the essence of a Secret Service that it must be secret, and if you once begin disclosure it is perfectly obvious to me as to honorable members opposite that there is no longer any Secret Service and that you must do without it. (Andrew, 1985, pp. 500–1)

Henry Brooke, Home Secretary in 1963, took the same line: 'The Security Service is, after all, a Secret Service. That is part of its essence.' (p. 500) After Philby's defection Harold Macmillan told MPs: 'it is dangerous and bad for our general and national interest to discuss these matters' (p. 500). Harold Wilson's work *The Governance of Britain* has a chapter barely a page long entitled 'The Prime Minister and National Security', which suggests it is only proper for prime ministerial responses to occasional questioning on security matters to be 'uniformly uninformative'. Edward Heath made it 'an inviolable rule' to refuse to publicize intelligence matters, and the Callaghan Government declared: 'Parliament accepts that accountability must be to Ministers rather than to Parliament, and trusts Ministers to discharge that responsibility faithfully' (pp. 500−1). The doctrine was re-affirmed by Douglas Hurd as Home Secretary in December 1988 when introducing the Security Service Bill and rejecting calls for parliamentary oversight: 'Secrecy is at the heart of security . . . It is actually fundamental to the success of the protection of the public by this service' (Hansard, 15 December 1988).

Yet despite the official policy there have been gaps through which information about this highly secretive world has filtered. Government decisions about the release of records and official histories have themselves been inconsistent. The four volumes of Professor F. H. Hinsley's official history of the role of British intelligence in 1939−45 have appeared in print, while Professor Michael Howard's official history of the role of deception in strategy and operations over the same period remains banned. Transcripts of wartime German intercepts have been released, but peacetime Soviet intercepts of the 1920s have been withheld indefinitely. When it comes to the question of publishing memoirs and other material in this field, there is an extremely chequered history of official opposition, ambivalence and quasi-encouragement. From time to time governments have been forced into publicly making exceptions to the rule of absolute secrecy. This has happened under great pressure in the wake of seriously embarrassing episodes, such as the Profumo and Blunt affairs, or when it has been seen as necessary to introduce legislation, as with the Interception of Communications Act and the Security Service Act.

We can now consider briefly to what extent government policy and these other sources have lifted the edges of the heavy veil of secrecy surrounding the various agencies and activities. Although its headquarters and training establishments have been identified together with many of its senior staff, the very existence of the SIS (or MI6 as it is still popularly known) *in peacetime* is still not officially acknowledged. When two of the organization's more notorious members were making headline news, the government issued special D-notices to the press to try to suppress references to the counter-espionage organization at the time of Kim Philby's defection and George Blake's trial for spying. Even when giving evidence on behalf of the British Government in an Australian

23

court during the Spycatcher trial in 1987, the Cabinet Secretary still refused to admit MI6 existed later than 1968. As for the Security Service (or MI5), officially it does exist, but the government refuses to discuss its role or operations in peacetime. Responsibility for the service was formally transferred from the Prime Minister to the Home Secretary in 1952, but this was not disclosed for eleven years. In 1963 a Conservative Government felt obliged to publish the report of an inquiry into the Profumo affair by Lord Denning; this made public for the first time the earlier change in ministerial responsibilities and the only acknowledged terms of reference for the service, issued in a letter now known as the Maxwell-Fyfe directive, dated September 1952 and sent by the then Home Secretary. After allegations of an earlier MI5 plot against the Labour Government of Harold Wilson emerged in the 1970s, the government held an internal inquiry and announced that no evidence had been found to support the allegations.

In recent years the policy of secrecy has come under a series of sustained attacks in Parliament and the press. The Bettany spy case in 1984 raised grave doubts about MI5's efficiency and security. The following year allegations made by Cathy Massiter and another former MI5 employee, about illegal activity (including unauthorized tapping of the telephones of Campaign for Nuclear Disarmament and trade union leaders) renewed calls for an independent inquiry and a system of genuine accountability to Parliament. *Spycatcher*, the memoirs of retired agent Peter Wright, were finally published in the UK in 1988, after prolonged legal action by the British Government had failed to stop publication and sale abroad. They revealed a picture of MI5's activities (with agents burgling and bugging their way across London and a reappearance of the Wilson plot allegations) which gave rise to renewed demands for greater political control and parliamentary oversight. Later that year the government introduced legislation, which for the first time put MI5 on a statutory basis.

Although the main role of GCHQ – interception of communications and decyphering or analysis of coded material and signals traffic – has remained the same, up until 1983 the government maintained a cover story, sticking firmly to the line that its task was research in telecommunications and the protection of British communications. The change of approach was brought about not by concern about the increasingly threadbare nature of the cover story but by the government's desire to introduce a ban on trade

24

union membership at GCHQ. As this decision, taken originally in 1981 after a period of industrial action in the Civil Service, was to be justified on grounds of national security, it became necessary first to acknowledge publicly GCHQ's primary purpose. This was done in distinctly low-key fashion by introducing a reference to its role in the interception of foreign communications in a written parliamentary answer on the case of the spy Geoffrey Prime.

Interception of private communications is one of the most sensitive areas of intelligence and state activity, and one which has been persistently kept from public scrutiny. There is evidence that the executive were opening letters as early as the sixteenth century. Two parliamentary secret committees set up after the Mazzini affair in 1844 conceded that by long usage the executive had acquired the power to intercept communications. Until 1985 there was no statutory basis for this. The practice and general extent of telephone tapping carried out under warrants issued by the Home Secretary was admitted to in the forty-page Birkett Report of 1957, set up after a row over the government's release of transcripts for private use by the Bar Council. Birkett recommended that the power should continue unchanged and that future figures should not be made public. Secrecy was restored until 1980 when, following embarrassing revelations in the Malone case of police interception of an antique dealer's telephone conversations, a terse eight-page White Paper was issued, giving a careful selection of statistics for the intervening period and setting out the 'safeguards' applied by the Home Secretary. (Neither report identified the actual numbers of telephones being tapped under the warrants listed or referred to any (presumably permanent) warrant to cover GCHQ's activities). However, a few years later the European Court of Human Rights found in the Malone case that the British Government's guidelines were in breach of the European Convention. This ruling led to the Interception of Communications Act 1985, which legalized the interception of post and telecommunications where the Home Secretary has issued a warrant on grounds related to national security, prevention or detection of serious crime, or safeguarding economic well-being. The new Act also established a tribunal with strictly limited functions: in the event of a complaint it is required merely to investigate whether a relevant warrant exists and it must also make an annual report to the Prime Minister. (This secretive ministerial monopoly can be compared with practice in West Germany where warrants are issued by a Parliamentary Commission and the person subject to tapping has eventually to be informed).

25

Questions about the overall control and co-ordination of the intelligence agencies are of course subject to the same absolute taboo on public or parliamentary debate, but there have been times when bland assurances from the three ministers concerned (the Prime Minister, the Home Secretary and the Foreign Secretary) have not been sufficiently persuasive and the government has had to make certain overt organizational changes. In 1964 after the Denning Report on the Profumo scandal, the Security Commission was established, chaired by a senior judge. Its role is simply to be available to carry out an inquiry if the Prime Minister should decide to refer a particular case to it. There is no commitment to publish the results of such inquiries, although the government may decide on partial publication, as with the 1985 report on the Bettany case. A 1984 Security Commission report on telephone tapping, produced by Lord Bridge, illustrates the merits of the system as a form of lightning conductor: it took him less than a week to review all 6,000 warrants issued over fifteen years and conclude that every single one was justified. Failures of intelligence assessment over Argentine intentions on the Falkland Islands in 1982 led to another major concession; the government had to grant hitherto unprecedented access to secret intelligence material for a select group of Privy Councillors under Lord Franks. Their report acknowledged the existence in peacetime of the Joint Intelligence Committee (the central Whitehall body for co-ordinating intelligence assessments). As a result of its recommendations the Committee was given an 'independent' Chairman, appointed by the Prime Minister. In November 1987, when faced by growing pressures for more effective oversight or at least an independent body for troubled staff to turn to, the government appointed a Staff Counsellor. He too has an essentially passive role carried out entirely behind the scenes: he is only required to report periodically to the three responsible ministers. So far the policy of absolute secrecy about funding and financial control (apart from the bald, partial figures of the Secret Vote) has been successfully maintained. The published vote for the secret services for 1988–9 was £113 million, and in December 1988 the Financial Secretary declined, in the interests of national security, to name other sources of funds. Unofficial estimates put the combined annual budget total at about £1 billion.

It is evident from this brief historical overview that the policy of absolute secrecy is neither inevitable nor sustainable, and over the years it has progressively lost credibility. The available evidence does not support the argument that a policy combining near total secrecy and non-accountability makes for good security and efficiency. There has been a catalogue of glaring failures, for instance in the security of overseas embassies between the wars, the string of Soviet moles and spy trials in the post-war period and the debilitating lack of effective inter-agency co-operation. The record of ministerial control remains one of Britain's better kept secrets, but all the indications are that interest has been sporadic and reactive, and control remote and unreliable. At one extreme there is a compulsive fascination with the arcane world of secret intelligence – as in Winston Churchill's case – and at the other a determined disinclination to probe into its murky affairs – as with the abstemious Arthur Henderson, who rated the Secret Service like hard liquor – he knew, and wanted to know, nothing of it. The Maxwell-Fyfe directive is noticeably more concerned with protecting the security services from political interference than with providing them with effective political supervision: ministers are essentially to be informed on a strictly 'need to know' basis.

The enormous glut of intelligence material produced by modern technology reinforces all the problems stemming from the inevitable isolation of those working in the agencies, inter-agency rivalry, unchallenged assumptions and entrenched positions that tend to flourish in any intelligence community. But all Western democracies, apart from Britain, have some form of external control over intelligence activities.

3 Secrecy and the Media

Along with the government's long standing desire to control the flow of information there has been an obsessive urge to influence its presentation. Both concerns have led to a close interest in the role of the media – press, broadcasting and publishing. On the one hand various means of managing the news and supplying the media with carefully processed material have developed: an extensive government public relations machine is supplemented by other more covert arrangements, notably the lobby system, itself kept secret for many years. On the other hand various forms of restraint have been imposed on the media, involving the use of both the criminal and the civil law and the adoption of certain mutually agreed practices, including the uniquely British phenomenon of the D-Notice Committee. What there has not been in Britain is a sustained tradition of freedom of the press as a principle which overrides other considerations. In the United States the first amendment to the constitution upholds the freedom of the press and the doctrine of no prior restraint applies. Under Swedish Freedom of the Press statutes it is unconstitutional for the government even to make inquiries about a newspaper's sources of government information. By contrast the British press is constrained in many different ways, including the Official Secrets Acts and the laws of confidence, contempt and libel. It has been described by one former editor, Cecil King, as 'censored in an arbitrary and indeterminate way' and by another, Harold Evans, as being only 'half-free'. This chapter examines how the government has sought to exercise control through official censorship, voluntary censorship and unofficial censorship. It also looks at the historical record of the government's recourse to the courts in its efforts to prevent or punish the appearance of certain press articles, broadcasts and books.

Official Censorship

Formal censorship in Britain has been applied on only a limited number of occasions. In wartime the need for some form of government censorship in the interests of national security has been generally recognized and accepted in Britain as in other Western democracies. A Press Bureau was set up in 1914 and in 1939—45 there was a Press Censorship Bureau within the Ministry of Information, which operated a quasi-voluntary system within a strict legal framework. In parallel, tight control was exercised over all the activities of the BBC. There was an understanding between the authorities and the media that no legal action would be taken against items that had been submitted to the official censor. While the need for censorship and self-restraint was accepted, there were many occasions when the press felt that the very wide-ranging rules were being applied in an unnecessarily restrictive and sometimes indiscriminate way. They objected to threats by the government, usually made after criticism of their handling of the war, to censor not just news but views. In 1940 after one episode the Government even used the police to investigate the share-holders of the *Daily Mirror*, one of their main critics. This wartime mentality re-emerged powerfully in 1982, when the peculiar circumstances of the Falklands campaign gave the government an effective monopoly of communications from the task force. Relations with the press suffered severe strain as a result of the strict controls imposed on both access and reporting and from instances of delay and dissembling.

Under the BBC's charter and the Broadcasting Act of 1981, the government has powers to issue directions about what may or may not be broadcast. Until recently these had not been formally invoked in peacetime, and it was assumed that they related only to a state of national emergency. However, in October 1988 Home Secretary, Douglas Hurd used these powers to impose a ban on interviews with members of Irish organizations which support violence.

Voluntary Censorship

The British tradition has been to rely on voluntary rather than formal methods of censorship. It was an early manifestation of the desire of the press to be seen as trustworthy that was one of the ingredients in the development of secret arrangements for the control of information negotiated in 1912. After 1898 the War Office had set in hand work on legislation to impose total press censorship in emergencies short of outright war. They commissioned a compliant freelance journalist, Sydney Brooks, to conduct a survey to assess the likely response of editors. The results dissuaded Whitehall from pressing ahead with that particular bill. Press hostility to the abortive move in 1908 to strengthen the OSA (by making unauthorized publication an offence) prompted Whitehall to approach things rather differently. The Director of Naval Intelligence suggested a new idea: 'a simple method, worthy of trial, is to put the press on their honour in the schoolboy sense of the term' (Palmer, 1984, p. 232). As he saw it, the press would be notified about things the department wanted to keep secret and asked to co-operate by not publishing information likely to be of value to foreign countries. This approach was not pursued immediately, as others were still keen to gag the press through legal means. A special CID sub-committee was set up under Churchill to review the prospects for legislation. Brooks again reported opposition and Churchill persuaded the committee to go for more subtle means. They endorsed the idea of a press bureau to be a purveyor of information and act in a friendly advisory capacity in order to secure a means of control. The War Office's subsequent approach to the Federation of Newspaper Owners was well received. Flattered by this show of trust, the proprietors readily agreed to form a joint committee and adopt a procedure for keeping material out of the newspapers. The idea was that the government representatives on this new body, to be called the Admiralty, War Office and Press Committee, would circulate Defence or 'D-Notices' among the press members before they were issued more generally to the press with a request to refrain from publishing information as indicated in the notice. From 1912 the committee operated to the satisfaction of both sides until interrupted by the outbreak of war.

An internal memo by the civil servant responsible for conducting the preliminary negotiations with the newspaper owners reveals the machiavellian thinking underlying the move. He pointed to the absence of any 'closely drawn definition of the scope of the new committee's powers and functions. This is not unintentional' (Palmer, p. 234). In explaining the objectives he had deliberately referred only to defence. 'The great point seemed to me to be to induce the Press to work together and in conjuction with us' (p. 234). He then went on to assess the prospects for using the 1911 OSA against the press. Legal advice suggested that 'in certain circumstances the Act could be used against a newspaper' (p. 234). The next passage again reveals the discrepancy between Whitehall's presentation of the Act and its real intentions:

> We have a note on our official papers to the effect that the
> speedy passage of the Act was due to a general understanding
> that the new measure was not directed against any new class,
> but against that which the former Act was aimed, viz the spy
> class, and that to use it against a newspaper merely for
> publishing news useful to an enemy would amount to a
> breach of faith with Parliament. But there is no record to
> this effect in the official versions of the debates. (p. 234)

Secrecy surrounded both the setting up and operation of the
new committee. In answering a parliamentary question in January
1913 Churchill merely mentioned the government had reason to
believe it could rely on the cordial co-operation of the press (p.
235). In September 1914 MPs were given a less than complete
description of the new system. They were told a committee had
been created, on which sat representatives of the War Office and
the Admiralty, to help achieve greater discretion in dealing with
'certain public matters'. On its operation they were told:

> indications were given . . . of the matters which, having regard
> to considerations of public convenience and interest, it was
> not thought desirable that the Press should deal with. That
> system continued until the outbreak of the war. (Williams,
> 1965, pp. 81–2)

This Admiralty, War Office and Press Committee was revived
after the war, but without publicizing the fact. An early example of
its use in the supression of non-defence matters was the D-
Notice issued to prevent press coverage of a trivial scandal relating
to Queen Alexandra's sister. In 1917 a D-Notice was issued to
ban references to industrial disputes and strikes. In a deliberate
move to extend the work of the committee to cover politically
sensitive items of foreign news, Foreign Office representation was
added. This official manoeuvre was executed in discreet, deliberately
low-key fashion by raising the idea at the end of a poorly attended
meeting and omitting any reference from the official minutes.
From 1923 for a period of twenty-three years the committee
remained in suspended animation; there were no further meetings
during this period, although existing notices remained in force and
new ones could still be issued.

After the Second World War and the abolition of formal censorship the committee was given a new lease of life under a new title, the Defence, Press and Broadcasting Committee. From 1946 its secretary came from the armed forces rather than the Press Association and the press was represented not by proprietors but by editors. The basic ingredients remained the same. The official notes accompanying the complete set of D-Notices as issued to newspapers keep up the original pretence. They state 'The D-Notice system is entirely voluntary and has no legal authority... it depends on goodwill and in effect very little else' (*New Statesman*, 4 April 1980). This 'very little else' is the threat of prosecution under the OSA in the event of failure to comply with the guidance. This threat appears to have come more to the fore from this time. The new secretary after 1946, Admiral Thomson, former Chief Press Censor, encouraged editors to ring him up for advice, and indicated that if he had passed a piece he would be prepared if necessary to make this clear in court. The committee's existence remained secret until 1952 and not until 1962 were details of how it operated made public (in the Radcliffe Report). This was the result of an inquiry set up after two controversial incidents in 1961, when abortive attempts were made to suppress information relating to George Blake's trial for espionage and to introduce a D-Notice which would have allowed only officially released information on all military weapons and equipment to be published, thereby stopping criticism of rapidly rising costs and extensive delays.

The D-Notice Committee, as it is popularly known, survived both public disclosure and the review. Radcliffe found a high level of press compliance, thought the committee made a valuable and effective contribution to protecting defence secrets and recommended its retention − provided it was not subject to abuse. This contrasts with the contemporary remarks of a former editor of *Aeronautics* magazine, who believed the committee's grim and efficient method of censorship prevented informed criticism of defence measures. Developments over the next twenty years were to impose renewed strains on the system and lead to a gradual breakdown of the consensus necessary to its continued effectiveness as a means of restraint. A series of clumsy government attempts to prohibit the disclosure of merely embarrassing aspects of espionage cases proved generally counterproductive. In 1967 came a further erosion of goodwill with the extraordinary 'D-Notice Affair', when the Wilson government was seen as pursuing a personal vendetta against the committee's right-wing secretary and the press took sides against the government. Mutual trust was dealt a further serious blow with the prosecution of journalist Jonathan Aitken and the editor of the *Sunday Telegraph*, Brian Roberts, in 1970 — despite previous clearance of their story about British arms supplies during the Nigerian civil war with the committee secretary. The *New Statesman* openly challenged the validity of what it termed 'the D-Notice quangette' in 1980 and the House of Commons Defence Committee decided to hold its own inquiry. Evidence from the press varied: one witness described the committee as a dangerous anachronism, whereas another wanted it preserved as long as possible as a quaintly British institution. While admitting that the system was failing to fulfil its role of maintaining confidentiality, the Select Committee concluded it should be retained at least until a fundamental review of the operation of the Official Secrets Act.

Today the system is still in place, but not all of the players are obeying the rules. The deference and club spirit which made it work in the early years have faded. Some editors prefer to make their own judgements about how far they can go without endangering national security. The protection ostensibly afforded to those who do take the precaution of consulting the relevant authorities looks even more dubious after an episode in 1987, when the government obtained an injunction to prevent the broadcast of a radio programme, *My Country Right or Wrong*, after the BBC had already sought and obtained clearance from the secretary of the D-Notice Committee. Yet both parties continue to subscribe to this covert form of voluntary censorship, despite its clearly reduced value as a means of ensuring secrecy on request. Provisions introduced in the 1989 OSA (see chapter seven), aimed at unauthorized *publication* rather than mere receipt, are designed to restore the position which the government had originally hoped to achieve at the beginning of the century — a façade of co-operation backed up by effective legal sanctions.

The development of the lobby system, another uniquely British institution, has a number of features in common with the evolution of the D-Notice Committee. An atmosphere of secrecy still surrounds its activities although its rules were leaked in 1970. A long tradition of observing an agreed code has in recent years shown signs of breakdown, but the system remains in operation. The 'lobby' started as a group of journalists who frequented the lobby of the House of Commons collecting political gossip. From 1884, after a series of Fenian explosions, the Serjeant at Arms started to keep a list of those privileged to mingle with MPs in areas banned to the public. By the end of the century it had become an established institution and lobby journalists had been transformed into an outlet for government information. The golden rule of the lobby is 'non-attribution'. A highly organized system of collective briefings takes place daily for about 150 accredited journalists, but officially these briefings do not exist and the sources are not to be mentioned by name. According to the lobby's code, a correspondent's primary duty is 'to protect his informants, and care must be taken not to reveal anything that could lead to their identification'. Stories obtained in this way are routinely but inadequately disguised by references such as 'sources close to the Prime Minister' or 'senior Whitehall sources'. The lobby's self-imposed rules of conduct require total secrecy: 'Don't talk about lobby briefings before or after they are held, especially in the presence of those not entitled to attend them' (Cockerell, 1984, p. 242).

The lobby has come under criticism as an outdated relic, a dishonest and mutually corrupting arrangement, unworthy of a modern democratic society and a genuinely free press. Public disclosure has not, however, altered very much. In 1984 lobby journalists celebrated their centenary with a lunch at the Savoy attended by the Prime Minister, a token of the lobby's continuing importance for politicians in news management. The system has spawned a series of specialized correspondents' 'lobbies', groups of trusted journalists prepared to work in close co-operation with particular government departments on the basis of informal contacts and unattributable or off-the-record briefings as well as formal press releases and conferences. However, a number of newspapers, the *Guardian*, the *Independent* and the *Scotsman*, no longer participate in the lobby system. In March 1987 the lobby itself reviewed the policy of non-attribution and voted by a narrow majority to continue the practice. As with the D-Notice system, most British newspapers remain reluctant to depart from long-established traditions of voluntary censorship.

Unofficial Censorship

The nature of unofficial censorship makes it even more difficult to trace the history of this third category of government restraint on the media. It is not the sort of activity that either side would normally want to become public knowledge. There is a strong

34

element of self-imposed restraint being exercised by the media themselves, for example in response to unwritten assumptions about political acceptability or to nods and winks transmitted through the old boy network of the British establishment. Lord Reith, the first Director-General of the BBC, made a revealing diary entry on the relationship between the government and the corporation at the time of the 1926 General Strike: 'they know they can trust us not to be really impartial' (Stuart, 1975, p. 96). It is clear, however, that there are occasions when governments see a need to intervene more forcefully behind the scenes and exercise some form of direct pressure in order to censor part or all of a programme or article. According to an investigative journalist who has provoked such pressures, unpublicized bullying beforehand is always a much more effective censorhip tactic than efforts at revenge after the event.

Although the BBC is supposed to be independent, there have been occasional glimpses of the application of government pressure. They reflect something of the ambivalent relationship between ministers and the corporation that is inherent in the way the BBC is organized and funded. To provide for the independence of the BBC it was established under royal charter, but this document also gives the Home Secretary formal powers of veto and the power to revoke its licence. The fact that the government controls the licence fee and appoints the Board of Governors inevitably creates the risk of undue political influence. A vital part of the case for the Home Secretary's powers is of course the government's responsibility for national security. Like the rest of the media the BBC is subject to the OSA and it is represented on the D-Notice Committee. However, a number of incidents indicate that successive governments have secretly resorted to various forms of censorship that were not directly motivated by the requirements of national security. For example only in 1986 did it emerge that since 1937 it had been the practice for BBC staff, on appointment or promotion, to be politically vetted by MI5. After the story appeared in the *Observer* the BBC undertook to restrict the extent of vetting to security-sensitive posts. In April 1937 the BBC and the Foreign Office came to an agreement under which the BBC would provide advance information about programmes on foreign affairs, including details of scripts and speakers, and the Foreign Office would offer 'any observations they might think fit, as to the convenience of the occasion proposed for such broadcasting, the general method of treatment, and the suitability of the speakers proposed' (*Listener*,

13 January 1989). The agreement was then used to prevent a talk by a Labour MP on Germany and to stop the Conservative and National Labour MPs Leo Amery and Harold Nicolson taking part in a discussion programme on the same subject. When Reith asked the Foreign Secretary point blank whether the government did wish to stop the two MPs, Lord Halifax told him this was the case but he would deny it if challenged in public (Listener, 13 January 1989).

The inside story of how the BBC came to ban Peter Watkins's film, *The War Game*, in 1965 provides a rare insight into the process of unofficial censorship at work. The proposal to make a film about the aftermath of nuclear war — and the risk of controversy — were accepted by the BBC in 1963:

> so long as there is no security risk, and the facts are authentic, the people should be trusted with the truth ... the film is bound to be horrifying and unpopular ... but surely necessary'. (Campbell, 1983 p. 89)

Filming went ahead, although the Home Office refused all co-operation. When the film was complete Lord Normanbrook (Chairman of the Board of Governors and a former Cabinet Secretary) secretly called in a panel of senior government officials to see the film and then wrote to tell Hugh Greene, the Director-General of the BBC, that 'Whitehall will be relieved if we do not show it' (Campbell, 1983, p. 89). The official view was that the film 'whatever its intention' would lend support to CND. Normanbrook's reply in September 1965 to Burke Trend, his successor as Cabinet Secretary, reveals a certain ambivalence. While describing the film as a 'purely factual statement ... based on careful research into official material', he warned it might well have 'a significant effect on public attitudes towards the policy of the nuclear deterrent' (Campbell, 1983, p. 90). In November Hugh Greene announced a ban on showing *The War Game*:

> This is the BBC's own decision. It has been taken after a great deal of thought and discussion but not as a result of outside pressure of any kind ... The film [was] too horrifying for the medium of modern broadcasting. (Campbell, 1983, p. 89)

In parallel with this less than frank statement from the BBC the

36

Home Office was giving journalists off-the-record briefings to the effect that psychologists anticipated a wave of 20,000 suicides if the film were shown. However, the film was shown in cinemas round the country and has been used by civil defence groups for training purposes. After a gap of about twenty years it was eventually transmitted by the BBC in 1986.

Resort to the Law

Censorship in its various forms is about prevention, but there are of course occasions when things slip through the net. In order to punish offenders and, most important, to deter others from following suit, the government has from time to time made use of both the criminal and the civil law against the media. Indeed the background to the 1911 OSA makes it clear that a major aim of the legislation was to put the government in a position where it could apply criminal sanctions to the press. Prosecutions under secrecy legislation have been brought against journalists under at least three different sections of the 1911 and 1920 Acts. The first cases in the 1930s involved the use of section 6, inaccurately presented to Parliament in 1920 as a measure directed against spies not journalists. This section made it an offence for someone to fail to give any information in their power about *any* offence or suspected offence under the OSA. In 1930 there was a leak in three newspapers about a Cabinet decision to arrest the Indian leader Mahatma Gandhi. The police started to question the journalists and proprietors concerned about their source, but the inquiry was called off when it was made clear that in the event of proceedings against them they would identify the Cabinet Minister responsible for the leak. This episode provoked a storm of protest in the press and assurances were again obtained from the government about the use of section 6 against the press.

Once again these proved worthless: in 1937 a journalist called Ernest Lewis was charged under section 6 for refusing to reveal his source for a story giving a description of a wanted man, clearly based on a police circular. In his defence Lewis argued he was being asked to do something in conflict with his professional code, which imposed a duty to protect his sources of information. He was found guilty and fined £5. Under renewed pressure (including a move by Dingle Foot MP to introduce amending legislation) the Home Secretary in May 1938 assured MPs the OSA would be confined to cases of 'serious public importance' and in December

37

he promised section 6 would be used only in cases of the gravest importance to the safety and welfare of the State. Only months later there was another attempt to use section 6, this time against a Conservative MP, Duncan Sandys (see chapter five). Breach of parliamentary privilege proved the final straw and the Official Secrets Act of 1939 was introduced to make the interrogation powers under section 6 apply only in espionage cases.

Use of section 2 against the press has also had a poor track record. On the relatively few occasions that prosecutions have been brought, the charges have been widely regarded as trivial or politically motivated. More numerous have been the reports of threatened use of the OSA to prevent or delay publication. The sheer absurdity of the circumstances has sometimes provided the newspaper with a good story. For instance in 1960 the editor of the *South East London Mercury* was warned that a story on trees blown down in a gale in Greenwich Park would contravene both the OSA and D-Notices. In 1948 a journalist named James Atkinson was found guilty and fined £10 on charges involving titbits of gossip passed on to him by a friendly telephone operator who had eavesdropped on local police calls. Although the Attorney-General defended the case as involving disclosure of information contrary to the public interest and assured MPs that proceedings were not initiated lightly, others were not convinced.

A prosecution brought as a result of an article published in the Oxford University magazine *Isis* in 1958 involved the highly sensitive topic of British monitoring of Soviet communications. The authors, two undergraduates with experience of signals interception as part of their national service, felt they were pointing to flagrant breaches of international law and dangerous acts of deliberate provocation along the Soviet frontier, arguing this was 'irresponsibility bred and sheltered by the Official Secrets Act' and that the information was already published abroad and well-known to the Soviet authorities. Despite a concerted government campaign to prevent any more revelations about the role of GCHQ, the case ensured widespread international publicity for an otherwise obscure publication. The judge decided the defendants had committed 'an act of more or less youthful folly' and sentenced them, far more leniently than expected after a largely in camera trial, to three months' imprisonment – to be backdated by two months and served 'in the most favourable circumstances...away from criminals' (Hooper, 1987, p. 82). Throughout, the police, the judiciary and the prison authorities seem to have been at pains to treat the pair as young gentlemen rather than mere journalists or real criminals.

Two of the famous cases described in chapter five involve journalists: the Aitken case in 1970 and the ABC case in the late 1970s. In different ways both served to discredit the use of the OSA against the press, not least because they were widely seen at the time as politically motivated prosecutions brought by an embarrassed government in the first case and a vindictive one in the second. In particular the decision in the ABC case to bring charges under section 1, so putting the gathering of information by a journalist on a par with spying, caused a huge outcry. In both cases the prosecution case turned out to have major weaknesses: in the Aitken case all four defendants were acquitted and in the ABC case after lengthy proceedings the section 1 charges were withdrawn and the three defendants received non-custodial sentences. Both cases raised the issue of press freedom and highlighted the scope for misuse of the OSA. There were no further attempts to use the legislation against the media. When Sarah Tisdall was sent to jail after sending documents to the *Guardian* in 1984, there was no prosecution against the editor for unauthorized receipt of official information.

In addition to the general deterrent effect of secrecy laws and D-Notices the government can also use the civil law to exercise prior restraint. Under British law a High Court judge may issue an injunction against publication if it is suggested that a forthcoming item is based on confidential information. The civil law of confidence has a number of advantages from the government's point of view: in the first instance an injunction can be obtained, often without any notice to the other side, in a private hearing before a judge. A successful application for a temporary injunction can be turned into a permanent ban on publication. An injunction obtained against one organization applies to the whole of the media. The publishers can be compelled to reveal the contents of their book and possibly the source, if they wish to have the injunction lifted. Successive governments have used the civil law of confidence to censor publication, but practice has been erratic and contradictory.

Considerable latitude has been given to ministers. Lloyd George and Churchill published with impunity multi-volume war memoirs which used vast amounts of official documents. Yet smaller fry, such as author Compton Mackenzie and Edgar Lansbury, son of a Cabinet Minister, ended up in court charged under section 2 (see chapter five). After the Second World War official attitudes to books about the security and intelligence services were also inconsistent. For example in 1955 Sir Percy Sillitoe, head of M15 from 1945−53, was permitted to publish his memoirs, *Cloak without Dagger,* with a foreword by a former Prime Minister. Yet this coincided with strenuous if ultimately unsuccessful attempts by the War Office to prevent former intelligence officer Colonel Alexander Scotland from publishing his book *The London Cage* about the interrogation of German prisoners of war. During the 1960s and 1970s other works also slipped through the net − where the authors were persistent or imaginative enough to stop endless haggling with Whitehall departments or the D-Notice Committee and resort to American publishers, or prominent intermediaries with good security service connections, or a ghost writer.

The prospect of revelations in a book called *GCHQ, the Negative Asset: the Failure and the Cover-Up* by Jock Kane provoked the government to obtain an injunction in 1982. Kane had taken early retirement after working for many years as a radio operator and waging an unsuccessful internal campaign to expose security weaknesses and corruption in Cheltenham and GCHQ stations round the world. His allegations had already featured in an ITV programme and an article in the *New Statesman* in 1980, but use of the civil law of confidence was clearly preferred to criminal proceedings (which would normally take precedence). The book remains unpublished. Publication has been allowed of numerous accounts of the activities of the security and intelligence services on the grounds that they were not written by intelligence officers, although authors such as Chapman Pincher and Nigel West (Conservative MP Rupert Allason) have clearly had major assistance from intelligence officers and highly sensitive subjects are described. Yet here too practice has been erratic. For instance in 1982 the government obtained an injunction against the second volume of Nigel West's account of Security Service Operations, having ignored the first volume covering the period up to 1945. However, faced with imminent publication in the United States and the *Sunday Times*' offer to meet West's legal expenses, publication was permitted after the removal of some agents' names.

The confused and apparently haphazard approach to publications in this field did not prevent the British Government in 1985 from pursuing a whole series of injunctions under the law of confidence against Peter Wright, his publishers and three British newspapers to prevent publication of *Spycatcher* (see chapter five). The government justified its prolonged, costly and ultimately unsuccessful legal campaign on the basis that it had to establish the principle that all employees of the security and intelligence services have a lifelong duty of confidentiality. The previous record of government policy on books written or contributed to by other such employees did much to undermine the government's case. A belated concern with consistency may well have prompted the injunction obtained against *My Country Right or Wrong* as the programme was on the topical issue, highlighted by Wright's book, of oversight of the security services. The offending programme was later broadcast, but only after the BBC had agreed to the unprecedented step in peacetime of providing the government with an advance copy of the script for them to censor. In another famous case, also discussed in chapter five, the Wilson Government used the law of confidence in 1975 in an attempt to establish the principle of Cabinet confidentiality and prevent publication of the Crossman diaries.

4 The Culture of Secrecy

Britain has fostered a culture of secrecy, which extends far beyond central government in many different and often unsuspected ways. Dick Crossman, Labour Cabinet Minister and commentator on the British constitution, once called it the real British disease. Secrecy is bolstered not just by the Official Secrets Acts but by over 100 other statutes which prohibit disclosure of information. While all democracies set limits on the extent to which their citizens can have access to government records and other information about the goods and services they pay for and the environment they live in, in area after area in Britain, from an early period right up to the present day, we find a low value placed on openness and a high priority attached to maintaining confidentiality. The motives behind all this secrecy do not always turn out to coincide with the public justification. Common themes emerge from the areas considered in this chapter: a fear of exposing mistakes; a desire to preserve exclusivity and professional mystique; a preference for providing public relations material rather than raw data, and a distrust of independent review of technical information. Despite often dire warnings of the consequences of allowing greater openness, the historical record (and the experience of other countries with more open systems) repeatedly shows that such predictions are unfounded.

Executive and Cabinet Secrecy

The desire for secrecy is an automatic reflex in the executive, but in Britain there are few checks to counter this impulse and the government has been able to set its own rules on how much information to give both Parliament and the public. Britain's extensive secrecy laws do not *require* government secrecy, but they have served to legitimize the practice. They were introduced to reinforce an already well-established doctrine and practice of executive secrecy. The justification provided for this policy of closed government is that the whole *process* of government must remain secret in order to ensure 'good government'.

The principle of Cabinet secrecy follows on from the general concept of government as an essentially private affair, but it is also justified as essential to preserve the convention of collective Cabinet responsibility. This doctrine has its origins in the need to protect individual ministers (orginally members of the king's privy council) from arbitrary interference by the monarch. It became a generally accepted convention from the mid-nineteenth-century, and has now been extended to include junior ministers and parliamentary private secretaries. Any minister wishing to voice public dissent from government decisions is expected to resign. Only rarely have temporary exceptions to the rule been permitted (for example on votes for women under Asquith or EEC entry under Wilson). All Cabinet Ministers and other senior ministers are still sworn in as Privy Counsellors for life. The oath (which dates back to the thirteenth-century and has been described as Britain's oldest secrecy provision) commits them to keep all advice to the monarch secret. In theory this means the secrets of the Cabinet room can only be divulged with royal assent and it was formerly the custom for a minister resigning on a point of principle to apply for the monarch's consent to explain publicly his reasons, as happened for instance with the resignations from the Balfour Government in 1903.

Until 1916 it was the accepted practice, reflecting the traditional view of Cabinet decisions as private advice to the monarch, to keep no formal record of Cabinet meetings apart from a letter from the Prime Minister to the monarch. When this proved a hopelessly inadequate way to run a world war, Lloyd George set up a Cabinet secretariat to co-ordinate, monitor and record the business of the Cabinet and its committees. While the minutes of Cabinet meetings taken by the first two Cabinet Secretaries, Maurice Hankey and Edward Bridges, provided a fairly full record of the discussion and attributed views to individual ministers, from 1946 under Norman Brook and his successors the style became terse and uninformative, giving no idea of individual views.

According to the rules a minister must obtain the assent of the monarch, advised by the Prime Minister, before going into print about his experiences. In practice this means negotiating with the Cabinet Secretary, as in the case of *No End of a Lesson* by Anthony Nutting, who had resigned as Minister of State in the Foreign Office at the time of the Suez crisis of 1956. Even in 1967 Sir

Burke Trend wanted to excise almost everything controversial and remove whole sections revealing what had really gone on behind the scenes, in particular details of Britain's collusion with France and Israel to attack Egypt. In the end Harold Wilson took a more relaxed view of disclosures about the Eden government and the book emerged with only a few omissions. This relaxed view did not apply to disclosures about his own administration. After the unsuccessful attempt to prevent the posthumous publication of volume I of the Crossman Diaries, the government set up the Radcliffe Committee to review the question of ministerial memoirs. Their report identified two guiding principles as laid down by Attlee in 1946: publication should not injure foreign relations or be useful to an enemy and it should not be destructive of the confidential relations on which the British system of government is based. The report implicitly acknowledged the artificiality and sheer impracticality of insisting on Cabinet secrecy since it suggested that ministers (unlike civil servants) may release some information because they are responsible for policy and need to defend their actions against public comment. Recognizing that no fixed principles of legal enforcement had emerged from the Crossman case, the committee concluded that the only real deterrent against ministers going too far was a sense of obligation to their colleagues and ex-colleagues (Cmnd 6386).

Flourishing alongside the theory of Cabinet secrecy there has of course been another powerful tradition in British politics — Cabinet leaks. Joseph Chamberlain recorded in his diary how a meeting of Gladstone's cabinet in the early 1880s had held a warm discussion on the subject of communication between Cabinet ministers and the press.

Limits of Accountability

According to British constitutional theory, Parliament is sovereign. In practice MPs come up against the powerful barrier of executive secrecy, bolstered in this context by the convention, again dating from the nineteenth century, that a minister is *personally* responsible to Parliament for the work of his department. Under the British system this also makes him responsible for decisions about what information can be released to Parliament. Although in this era of vastly expanded departmental responsibilities it is no longer feasible for a minister to exercise effective control over the bulk of the activities of his civil servants, he can still control the flow of information provided to MPs through answers to parliamentary questions and the evidence presented to Select Committees.

Ministers can, and habitually do, reply to parliamentary questions with a minimum of information. Only about one-third of questions put down for oral reply are answered in that way, and the questioner is limited to one supplementary question. Ministers may decline to answer on grounds that the information is not readily available or could only be acquired 'at disproportionate cost'. There is moreover a long list of topics on which they refuse to answer altogether. The ministerial right to refuse to reply was firmly established by a Speaker's ruling in 1893. The existence of a blacklist − those topics on which MPs are not allowed to ask questions − was itself kept secret until 1972. It came to light in the course of a parliamentary inquiry into 'question packing', an unofficial practice (involving planting favourable questions with party loyalists to avoid more intrusive questioning) which had itself only been revealed in a memo leaked to the *Sunday Times*. The ninety-five forbidden subjects listed in the ensuing report include many oddities, ranging from the activities of the White Fish Authority through agricultural workers' wages and aircraft accident rates to forecasts of unemployment and food prices.

To provide more effective means of parliamentary scrutiny a system of specialized Select Committees was introduced in the mid-1960s, although not until 1980 did each Whitehall department have a committee to monitor its work. But even these committees have limited powers, and sometimes limited inclinations, to probe into matters against the wishes of the minister concerned. According to the instructions for civil servants giving evidence (known as the Osmotherly rules) 'any withholding of information should be limited to reservations that are necessary in the interests of good government or to safeguard national security'. But officials are warned to take into account 'the risk of publication' when deciding what to make available and the list of areas to be withheld from MPs in the interests of 'good government' is a long one. It includes advice given to ministers, information about inter-departmental exchanges, consultations between ministers and information about Cabinet committees and Whitehall review procedures.

Secrecy and the Civil Service

The need for lifelong secrecy about their work is brought home to all civil servants from the time they join the service. They are required to sign form E74, which means declaring that they have read and understood the provisions of the OSA and giving an undertaking in respect of publication:

> I am aware that I should not divulge any information gained by me as a result of my appointment to any unauthorised person, either orally or in writing, without the previous official sanction in writing of the Department appointing me, to which written application should be made and two copies of the proposed publication forwarded. I understand also that I am liable to be prosecuted if I publish without official sanction any information I may acquire in the course of my tenure of an official appointment (unless it has already been made public)... (Ponting 1985, pp. 36–7)

Although the requirement to submit two copies of any publication is purely an administrative one, the method of presentation is clearly designed to give the impression that it too has legal backing. In fact this initiation ceremony, known as 'signing the Official Secrets Act', has no legal force; everyone is bound by the Act whether they sign the form or not. Describing the impact of section 2, one senior civil servant told the Franks Committee: 'at the back of everything you say and do all day long there is this tremendous sanction' (Wilson, 1984, p. 15).

The importance of secrecy is reinforced in many other ways, both formal and informal. The process of negative vetting (a check against Special Branch and MI5 files) applies to all entrants and a much more detailed investigation known as positive vetting is applied to those occupying a large range of posts, many of which have nothing to do with defence or national security. Similarly, an elaborate system for classifying and special handling of documents applies throughout the service. Supposedly based on the damage that release would cause to the nation, the four basic categories run from Restricted (undesirable in the interests of the nation) through Confidential and Secret to Top Secret (exceptionally grave damage to the nation). There is no clear guidance on applying classifications and what happens in practice is over-classification and pervasive abuse of security markings to reinforce the protection of politically sensitive or potentially embarrassing information. In the absence of any general procedures laid down for obtaining authorization, the tendency is to play safe. All civil servants are trained to adopt a cautious approach, to be wary of letting outsiders, including MPs, know too much. Instructions issued after the Ponting case (see chapter 5), known as the Armstrong memorandum, direct anyone with moral qualms to pass 'the burden of conscience' on to his permanent secretary. A civil servant's duty of confidentiality is thus made into an absolute and inflexible rule.

Parliamentary Secrecy

Parliamentary secrecy is one tradition that has not survived intact, although there was a prolonged rearguard action to try to preserve the principle. Like so many other constitutional conventions this long outlived its original purpose, which was to prevent interference by the Crown. Until the late-nineteenth-century the House of Commons maintained a formal ban on the reporting of its debates and repeatedly condemned the growth of clandestine reporting and unofficial reports as a breach of parliamentary privilege. Until the 1970s the record of parliamentary debates could not be used in court cases without a specific vote by Parliament. (In the United States the House of Representatives has always met in public and the Senate has done so since 1794.) Even today Parliament retains its right to exclude 'strangers' and to hold secret sessions, as it did on occasion during both world wars.

Access to Public Records

Not until 1958 was there legislation to establish a general policy on access to government records. Before then the basic principle was non-disclosure, although individual government departments set their own rules for granting limited access. In 1899 an MP declared:

> on the general question of keeping documents secret there is no country in Europe which is so scrupulous and old-fashioned in imposing secrecy upon its public documents as is this country. (Williams, 1965, p. 65)

The debate followed a complaint by an Irish MP refused access to documents held in Dublin Castle on the Irish rebellion of 1798. Even where historians were concerned, practice varied greatly. In 1898 it transpired that an author writing a history of the period

47

1793–1815 had been allowed access by the Foreign Office but could not go beyond 1800 in the Home Office papers.

The system was reviewed by the Grigg Committee, which reported in 1954. Based on its recommendations the government introduced a fifty-year rule in the Public Records Act of 1958; records would normally be opened after fifty years, with government discretion to extend or reduce this period. The choice of period was largely justified by Grigg as preventing civil servants being embroiled in political controversy and enabling them to maintain frankness and 'unselfconsciousness' in the knowledge that what they wrote would not be available for public inspection during their lifetime. In the committee's view:

> The susceptibilities of the individual in this respect are not less important than the natural desire of the historian to obtain his material as soon after the event as possible. (Cmd 9163)

What preoccupied Conservative Cabinet Ministers presented with the Grigg report was the prospect of official disclosure of Cabinet records during their lifetime; they were most reluctant to concede the proposal, even when assured that the new arrangements would still make it possible to keep back documents to avoid 'embarrassing consequences' and that Crown copyright would prevent quotation at any length. Two years later they readily agreed on the need to retain some types of records indefinitely and to draft the legislation so that each *government department* would have the right to 'withhold any documents or classes of documents which they consider unsuitable for release'. Having decided to grant access after fifty years to departmental records subject to such safeguards it took them two more Cabinet meetings to agree that the same should apply to Cabinet records. Their discussion throws an interesting light on why modern Cabinet minutes are so reticent about the exchange of personal views: it is the price paid for eventual public access. In December 1957 Macmillan's Cabinet was assured that 'the impersonal style in which Cabinet discussions were recorded should protect members of the Cabinet from the disclosure of individual views which might be embarrassing even after fifty years' (PRO CAB 128/31 CC(57) 86th Conclusions).

In response to calls for a more realistic period, the 1958 Act was amended in 1967 to introduce the current thirty-year rule. The legislative provisions and the administrative arrangements still allow individual departments a major role in determining what records are destroyed (an estimated 99%), retained or released to the Public Record Office (PRO). In 1958 responsibility for the PRO (set up in 1838) was transferred from a senior judge to a government minister, the Lord Chancellor. He has powers to approve the retention by departments of whole classes of records as well as individual items and to give 'blanket approvals' for *all* records relating to particular subjects on any departmental file to be withheld. In 1986 there were three such blanket approvals in force: records of intelligence and security matters (granted in 1967) and two others granted in 1979 covering records of civil and home defence planning for 1946−55 and all Cabinet and Cabinet committee records on atomic energy and overseas defence planning.

The list of records retained by departments on administrative or other special grounds throws up some unexpected areas of persistent official secrecy, including files on land drainage and historical monuments in Wales, the records of the British Pharmacopoeia Commission from 1930, plans of the Forest of Dean from 1833 and agricultural returns summarized by parish after 1918. There is also a category of 'statute-barred' records. Certain acts, from the Corn Production Act of 1917 to the Agricultural Statistics Act of 1979, prohibit absolutely the release of information collected under their provisions. Records that are transferred to the PRO may still be subject to 'extended closure', although the public may inspect the document conveying the Lord Chancellor's instrument of approval and the schedule of file titles affected. Reasons for extended closure relate to certain types of personal information, information supplied in confidence and the very widely drawn category of 'exceptionally sensitive papers, the disclosure of which would be contrary to the public interest whether on security or other grounds' (PRO Information Sheet No. 37 1986). Included in the latter category, for example, are papers on the abdication crisis of 1936, which are closed for 100 years. It remains possible to grant 'privileged access' to certain records otherwise unavailable but only subject to an undertaking (which will usually involve submitting a draft for official approval). There have even been instances when files previously available for public inspection are suddenly removed from the PRO, as happened for instance with discussions on Britain's claim to the Falkland Islands, which disappeared in 1982. Whereas many other countries have decided to pass legislation to allow early access to all but a few carefully defined categories of contemporary government papers, in Britain the concept of public records still appears to be something of a misnomer.

Secrecy and the Courts

Official secrecy also impinges significantly on the process of civil law. British citizens seeking access to government documents relevant to legal proceedings come up against the doctrine of Crown privilege, now known more euphemistically as Public Interest Immunity. The Crown can plead public interest as a reason for refusing to disclose document material to a case, whether or not the Crown is itself a party to the proceedings. Under the British adversarial legal system this withholding of information can have a significant impact on the outcome, since judge and jury are only required to be arbiters of what is placed before them; they have no responsibility for ensuring the evidence is complete. What has been at issue is how far a judge can challenge a ministerial decision to claim immunity. In 1942 the House of Lords ruled that a ministerial objection to disclosure on grounds of public interest was conclusive. The relevant judgment allowed a very broad interpretation of public interest, going beyond national security and diplomatic relations to take in cases 'where the practice of keeping a class of documents secret is necessary for the proper functioning of the public service' (Williams, 1965, p. 194). However, in 1968 the Law Lords modified their earlier decision. While a citizen bringing a legal action still has no right to see all the relevant evidence, the decision as to whether to accept a ministerial certificate may now be decided on a case by case basis. In a few cases the courts have started to examine the case for secrecy more critically than in the past. In one case the judge actually read all the documents concerned before pronouncing them not sufficiently relevant to warrant disclosure. This is another area where British legal practice may be moving slowly towards accepted practice under administrative law elsewhere, which does not automatically assume the propriety of the government's motives for secrecy.

Local Government Secrecy

The process of reforming local government in Britain began in the 1830s, and secrecy emerged as an issue towards the end of the century. A legal decision that reporters had no right to attend council meetings led to legislation in 1908 to allow the press access. However, it proved inadequate and local councils found it easy to get round its provisions. This early experience of legislative reform to open up local government followed by evasive action on the part of the authorities to preserve secrecy was to be repeated.

After various unsuccessful attempts to bring in a private member's bill, a Conservative backbencher called Margaret Thatcher managed, despite front bench opposition, to get enacted her Public Bodies (Admission to Meetings) Act 1960, which was aimed at opening up council meetings to both press and public. The government's objections were that such a move would be too costly and would inhibit the necessary candour between elected representatives and officials — arguments that would also feature strongly in the case against greater openness in central government. Since the new Act continued to allow secrecy if the council deemed it 'prejudicial to the public interest' and there was no enforcement machinery or penalties for evasion, many meetings were still held in secret. Provisions to provide for greater public access to information and meetings were included in the 1972 Local Government Act, but only one provision (about disclosure of accounts) entailed a penalty. In effect it allowed the practice of transferring business from open committee meetings to closed sub-committee meetings. Subsequent surveys of local government practice have revealed a wide divergence in attitudes towards public access. In 1979 over half those surveyed were still holding committee meetings in secret and in 1984 all sixty-one councils covered were found to have in some way breached or evaded their statutory duty of disclosure.

In 1985 the Local Government (Access to Information) Act, a private member's bill, was passed with support from the government. Although originally intended to constitute a freedom of information measure for local government (something the government had already rejected out of hand for central government), the various exemptions still provide scope for a council to exercise its own judgement about release of documents. Another private member's bill has since provided an individual with the right of access to personal files held on him. This too received government backing but only on condition its provisions were confined to local government.

Secrecy and the Consumer

Outside government departments and town halls there are many different sorts of bodies which provide a wide range of goods and services. In their role as consumers, members of the public are paying for the end products, either directly as in the case of gas or electricity or indirectly through taxation, as with education or the health service; or else they are affected by the way that the goods and services are produced, by manufacturing safety standards for example, or the environmental impact of the processes involved. Yet there is no general principle of public accountability, no right of access to information. Only about half a dozen statutes provide for any form of mandatory disclosure, compared with the hundred or more prohibiting disclosure. The practice of secrecy is maintained by a powerful combination of factors, including the requirement to protect government information, voluntary secrecy agreements between the various parties, the desire to protect commercial information, and habit. Voluntary disclosure of information is widely seen by those on the inside as unnecessary, inconvenient and risky.

Even in the case of nationalized industries there is no particular onus on them to be forthcoming — public ownership does not imply public access. The juxtaposition of the OSA and commercial sensitivity produces a pervasive ethos of confidentiality. For example, in 1980 the electricity industry was found to have fourteen different types of secrecy markings, and a 1971 report on the effects of fluorescent light was classified as confidential. Even the consumer councils covering each industry find it difficult to penetrate the wall of secrecy. They remain uncomfortably dependent on the goodwill of the industry itself for a supply of information. Much of what they are told is on a confidential basis, and so cannot be used to support any case they might wish to make publicly on behalf of consumers and in opposition to the industry. Consumer councils themselves vary a good deal in their openness with the press, public and pressure groups.

Since the mid-nineteenth century the government has passed laws and set up agencies to control and monitor the effects of pollution. None of the acts aimed at controlling pollution make it a requirement for the general public to be told in the event of a health hazard, whereas virtually all of them restrict disclosure, often going far beyond the need to protect specific trade secrets. For instance the Public Health Act of 1936 protects data relating to 'any manufacturing process' and the Health and Safety at Work Act 1974 protects 'any information' obtained by an inspector using his powers under the Act. Indeed, if an inspector investigating under the 1968 Trade Descriptions Act comes across possible breaches of other legislation it would be illegal for him to pass the information to his colleagues or to let the author of a complaint know the outcome of his investigation. As public concern about environmental pollution has grown, the trend in legislative provision has been generally towards more, not less, secrecy. Since it was set up in 1863, the Alkali Inspectorate (which monitors industrial air pollution) has operated on the principle that all its information must be considered private unless demanded by law or permitted by the owner, but not until 1974 did this have legal backing. The 1983 Water Act removed the public right of access to meetings of water authorities granted under the 1960 Act. A revealing entry in the Crossman diaries suggests the balance of power within government departments that produces such legislation: 'nearly all my technical advisers were passionately in favour of the producer and against the amenity lobby' (Crossman, vol I, p. 311). The resulting imbalance produces a set of priorities that repeatedly put maintaining secrecy and commercial interests above preventing pollution or informing the public about hazards. For many years the Royal Commission on the Environment has criticized the extent of secrecy in this area, but there has been little progress. Under the Rivers (Prevention of Pollution) Act a company that pollutes a river can be fined, whereas an official revealing the information without the company's consent can be sent to prison for three months. In Britain control of pesticides is left to a voluntary agreement, and the price paid for the co-operation of pesticide manufacturers is a ban on the general release of information obtained about individual products submitted for testing and approval. Information about the performance of individual makes of car in British MOT tests is withheld in the interests of manufacturers rather than the public; for instance the public is permitted to know that 21 per cent of cars failed because of defective brakes, but not which makes of cars failed the tests due to defective brakes. The location of the great majority of the 1,500 sites handing dangerous chemicals in Britain is still treated as an official secret, and only those people living close to sites classified as major hazard sites have acquired the right to be informed, under an EEC directive which came into force in 1984.

Nuclear Secrecy

Nowhere has the national obsession with secrecy been more evident and persistent than in the case of Britain's nuclear programme. From the start the arrangements and attitudes surrounding the original top secret wartime military project were carried over to the civil industry. Work on all nuclear programmes was deliberately made the responsibility of a virtually autonomous body, the UK Atomic Energy Authority (UKAEA), and the provisions of the OSA were bolstered by special D-Notices and the Atomic Energy Act 1946, which makes disclosure of information a criminal offence. One D-Notice prevented the press from mentioning the purpose of the atomic weapons research establishment at Aldermaston until 1953. In 1962, when a committee was set up in Whitehall to discuss the choice of the next type of civil nuclear reactor, the Prime Minister refused to disclose its terms of reference or even to confirm its existence. Considerations of public health and safety have not been given precedence, and it was not until the 1970s that the government disclosed the true extent of the 1957 Windscale nuclear accident. Exceptions have also been granted to the thirty-year rule and in 1979 all Cabinet records on atomic energy were exempted from disclosure. In 1984 papers relating to key decisions on the establishment of a civil nuclear programme leading up to the 1954 White Paper remained closed for at least fifty years.

To some extent recent public inquiries that have accompanied the requests from the Central Electricity Generating Board (CEGB) for planning permission for new civil nuclear power stations have opened up a public debate. But the record of these lengthy and complex public inquiries reveals a still unequal struggle by those outside the nuclear industry for access to certain key elements of inside information, in particular data relating to safety aspects and the economic case. A request for a copy of the safety study for the 1974 Torness inquiry was turned down on the grounds that publication would not help the public, whose interests, it was argued, were fully safeguarded by the (nuclear) inspectorate. Despite the 100 kg of material produced by the CEGB for the Sizewell inquiry in the 1980s, opponents of the scheme were refused public funds to help them prepare their case and had to resort to using the American Freedom of Information Act to obtain access to research undertaken by the UKAEA into safety aspects of the proposed reactor. There are now moves to restrict exposure of the case against nuclear power in public inquiries, and resistance to disclosures about the whole process of decision-making shows few signs of weakening. In 1987, after examining the historical record, one commentator on secrecy in British Government said:

Nuclear decision-making seems to be an extreme form of the characteristic features of British government decision-making — that is secrecy, concealment, deception and forfeiture of trust. (Cornford, 1987, p. 190)

5 Use and Abuse of the Law: Famous Cases

Given the catch-all nature of section 2 of the 1911 Official Secrets Act, there were countless technical breaches of the law every day, but legal proceedings were relatively rare. The Franks Report traced thirty known prosecutions under this section, including twenty-six convictions, in the period up to 1972. Official figures for the thirty years to February 1985 cited fifty-two prosecutions leading to thirty-six convictions. This chapter looks at the general pattern of prosecutions under section 2 and features nine famous cases, including two involving the use of the civil law of confidence. The great majority of cases never made the headlines. It is difficult to identify a consistent rationale behind the cases that came to court, or the sentences handed out. Few official secrets trials had anything to do with national security; the information disclosed often turned out to be fairly trivial stuff. In some instances the disclosure caused no more than political embarrassment. Despite the supposed safeguard of the Attorney-General's personal sanction, on many occasions the prosecution case was made to look misconceived or ill-prepared or both. Worse still, the legal process itself was brought into disrepute and exposed to accusations of political abuse and bias as a result of those highly controversial trials that did make headline news.

A sizeable category of section 2 cases are in fact remarkable only for their triviality, at times verging on the ludicrous. They served as a periodic reminder that *any* unauthorized disclosure could attract criminal charges – perhaps this was their *raison d'être*. For example in 1926 a retired governor of Pentonville prison was fined £250 after revealing details of the last hours of a convicted murderer; in 1932 a Somerset House clerk and a *Daily Mail* reporter received prison sentences totalling fourteen weeks in a case involving the disclosure, in return for a small payment, of details of three wills a few hours before their official release; in 1946 two men were fined after a publication said one of them had been employed by military intelligence; in 1959 a young man just out of the navy showed some official documents to a friend, there was a citizen's arrest and he was fined and gaoled for one day. In 1984 a Home Office official was even charged with unauthorized disclosure to another Home Office official. The two documents in question contained technical details about a prison project for manufacturing toy typewriters. Following an unsuccessful attempt to withdraw the charges in the wake of the Ponting trial and the collapse of the prosecution case, the judge directed that the defendant be acquitted.

There is another broad category of cases where the defendants were guilty of not much more than carelessness or lack of judgement, but where the authorities have chosen, for reasons that are not always readily apparent, to use the criminal law rather than take internal disciplinary action. In 1951 three young men were fined for telling each other details of aircraft being produced at Farnborough where two of them worked. In 1961 an Admiralty clerk was charged with taking documents home to work on them without asking for permission. In 1981 a Ministry of Defence official, who had used official tapes for recording pop music, was charged with retaining official documents without authority and remanded on £5,000 bail before charges were finally dropped because the prosecution could not prove what was originally on the tapes. In 1983 a senior information officer was fined £500 after losing his briefcase on a London Underground train. Members of the armed forces had previously been court-martialled for similar offences under section 2, but this was the first case brought against a civil servant. Robin Gordon-Walker may have been singled out for such treatment because *City Limits* subsequently published the contents of his briefcase and he happened to be the son of a former Labour Foreign Secretary who had come in for criticism for revelations in his 1976 book entitled *The Cabinet*.

Another category of OSA prosecutions arguably need not or should not have involved use of the Act at all. Most of this type involved the corrupt use of official information, where other relevant laws or internal sanctions would have been more suitable. Examples include a civil servant fined in 1945 for giving information about tankers to a shipping broker; a policeman who offered information to the press during the Yorkshire Ripper case in 1981 and a police computer operator who passed on information to a burglar alarm company in 1984. There were also cases where charges under the OSA appear to have been used as a sort of makeweight or on a contingency basis – thrown in on top of the main charges brought under corruption, bankruptcy or other legislation.

Part of the controversy surrounding section 2 revolved round cases where, despite an apparently flagrant breach of the Act, no prosecution was brought. In respect of all cases under the OSA the discretion of the Attorney-General is absolute; there is no legal means of challenging his decision to proceed or not to proceed. No minister has ever been prosecuted under the 1911 Act. When in 1965 Dick Crossman left Cabinet papers in a fashionable West End restaurant, and they were then passed onto the *Daily Express*, the only threat of prosecution – intended to deter publication – was directed against the newspaper. After the Ponting acquittal in 1985 failure to use section 2 gave rise to controversy in the case of Cathy Massiter (involving allegations of illegal activity by MI5), in the Westland Affair (where the Attorney-General granted an indemnity against prosecution in advance of a purely internal inquiry into the leak of a controversial ministerial document) and in the Zircon Affair (where Special Branch raided BBC premises).

Instances abound of the threatened use of section 2, mostly recounted by editors or authors who nonetheless persisted in publication and called the authorities' bluff. While it is clear that the OSA is more frequently used to deter than to punish, what it takes to trigger off its use in a punitive way is far from clear, and it is this apparently random application which has done much to foster the belief that section 2 has frequently been abused. A series of famous cases also exposed the working of the law to critical examination, focused public attention on the motives for bringing a prosecution and highlighted the practice of executive secrecy.

The Trial of Compton Mackenzie

Anyone wanting to read the first edition of Compton Mackenzie's *Greek Memories* in Oxford's Bodleian Library must first apply to the Foreign Office for permission. Compton Mackenzie was a captain in the Royal Marines during the First World War and afterwards developed into a prolific writer. In 1932 he was planning to bring out the third volume of his wartime memoirs about his experiences in military intelligence in the Balkans. In it he was preparing to challenge an account by Sir Basil Thomson, a former Director of Intelligence, whose work *The Allied Secret Service in*

Greece had appeared in 1931. When (under MacDonald's national government) he was charged under section 2 of the OSA with unauthorized disclosures to his publishers, Mackenzie decided to contest the case. At the committal stage prosecution claims about the damage done in naming former intelligence officers were shown up in cross-examination as absurd and, to avoid further embarrassment, Mackenzie was offered a deal, which he accepted. If he changed his plea to guilty, the penalty was to be no more than a £500 fine and £500 costs. In fact the Attorney-General's inept handling of the case so irritated the trial judge that the outcome was a mere £100 fine and £100 costs. The judge was unimpressed by the allegation that Mackenzie had revealed that the Head of the British Secret Service was known as 'C' and that this dated from the days of its first chief, Sir Mansfield Cumming, since such facts were already well-known in the London clubs to which he and the Attorney-General belonged. In summing up he observed that no harm had come from publication, except possibly in one case, but the defendant should have obtained official permission. In an act of revenge for what he considered a needless and spiteful prosecution Mackenzie later wrote *Water on the Brain*, a savage satire on the Secret Service. He also tried to interest members of the Labour Shadow Cabinet in reforming section 2, but was told they could not help because they might want to use the Act when they were next in power.

The Trial of Edgar Lansbury

In 1934 Edgar Lansbury published a book called *Lansbury, My Father*. His father was George Lansbury, former Labour Cabinet Minister and at the time of the book's publication leader of the Labour Party. In conveying his father's views on social policy, Edgar Lansbury quoted from two Cabinet memoranda prepared in 1930–31. As a result he was charged under section 2 with unlawfully receiving information communicated to him in contravention of the OSA. No charges were brought against his father, and the prosecution avoided altogether the question of who was responsible for communicating the information in the first place. Edgar Lansbury was fined £20 and 25 guineas in costs. After the case the rule permitting ministers to retain Cabinet documents was changed. Like Lloyd George and Churchill, Lansbury refused to return his papers when requested to do so. This time Whitehall got its own back. Once the Treasury Solicitor got hold of thirty boxes of papers from Lansbury's executors in 1944 — ostensibly to sift out and keep back only secret documents — they were never returned and Lansbury's official biographer had to produce the *Life of George Lansbury* in 1951 without the confiscated papers.

The Duncan Sandys Affair

In 1938 Duncan Sandys was a Conservative backbencher and a second lieutenant in the Territorial Army. Like his father-in-law, Winston Churchill, he received inside information about the true state of Britain's military capabilities that conflicted with the government's public line. His concern about serious shortages of anti-aircraft guns around London was confirmed by secret figures passed to him by his adjutant. When he started to challenge assurances to the contrary from the Secretary of State for War in Chamberlain's government, to his amazement he found himself summoned to an interview with the Attorney-General, a move subsequently described by the Home Secretary as difficult to defend. An indignant Sandys immediately reported to the Speaker of the House of Commons that the Attorney-General had threatened him with use of section 6 of the OSA after he had refused to disclose his source. He had been warned that the penalty for failing to help inquiries under the Act was up to two years' imprisonment. Over the next few days there developed an embarrassing political row over the alleged use of the OSA in order to thwart a Member of Parliament carrying out his legitimate parliamentary activity. Despite receiving a denial and written assurances of no further action from the Attorney-General, Sandys referred the issue to the House of Commons Committee of Privileges. An infuriated War Office then tried a different tactic and summoned him to attend a military court of inquiry, but he refused to appear and immediately raised the matter in the House. The Committee of Privileges found both the military summons and the legal interview amounted to a serious breach of privilege, and strongly condemned the conduct of the Attorney-General and the lack of judgement shown by the Secretary of State for War. In the wake of this affair (which followed the controversial use of section 6 against the press in the Lewis case), the government introduced the Official Secrets Act 1939. Its sole purpose was to limit the special interrogation powers (which in effect removed an individual's right to remain silent) to espionage cases.

The Trial of Jonathan Aitken and Others: the Nigerian Arms Case

Under Harold Wilson's first Labour Government in 1970 a section 2 prosecution was brought following the publication of an official report about the Nigerian civil war. The offending document embarrassed both the Nigerian and British Governments, as it revealed not only corruption and waste in the Nigerian army but also that the Labour Government had been making misleading statements about the extent of British arms supplies to the federal government during the civil war. The trial was widely condemned as political, and the highly selective choice of defendants added to the prosecution's difficulties. A copy of the official document in question had been sent by the British defence adviser in Lagos to Colonel Cairns, then a member of the international observer team stationed in Nigeria, who had passed it on to his former superior, a retired Major-General, who had lent it overnight to a dinner guest, Jonathan Aitken (journalist and local Conservative parliamentary candidate), who in turn had sent copies to a former Conservative minister and, through his literary agent, to the *Sunday Telegraph*.

Charges were brought, however, only against Cairns, Aitken, the newspaper's editor and the newspaper itself. Because of the weakness of the prosecution case in establishing a chain of guilt, the defendants merely sketched in a public interest defence and the case for upholding the freedom of the press. Mr Justice Caulfield's summing up savaged the prosecution case and he went on to suggest it was time for section 2 to be pensioned off and replaced with a measure to provide greater clarity about what constituted an offence liable to prosecution. Despite the prosecution's disclaimer of any political motive, he commented: 'It may be that prosecutions under the Official Secrets Act can serve as a convenient and reasonable substitute for a political trial' (Hooper, 1987, p. 102). The four defendants were acquitted, and it was against this background of a seriously discredited section 2 that the Franks Committee prepared a report and in 1972 recommended its repeal and replacement.

The Crossman Diaries Case

In 1975 the Wilson Government sought an injunction against the literary executors of Richard Crossman to ban publication of volume I of *The Diaries of a Cabinet Minister*. Use of the civil law of confidence was evidently considered preferable to a prosecution under the OSA, since Michael Foot, one of Crossman's executors, was a Cabinet Minister at the time. The book dealt with events in 1964—6 when Crossman had been Minister of Housing and Local Government. Negotiations with the Cabinet Secretary had proved fruitless, since Sir John Hunt's position was that no details of Cabinet discussions, advice given by civil servants or conversations about policy between ministers could be published — precisely the aspects which Crossman had wanted to illustrate in his detailed day-by-day record of events. After substantial extracts of the diaries had appeared in the *Sunday Times*, the government's application was heard in July 1975 by Lord Widgery, the Lord Chief Justice. There was no question of national security; the question at issue was Cabinet confidentiality. The case produced a paradoxical result. Lord Widgery ruled that the expression of individual opinions by Cabinet Ministers was a matter of confidence, and the Crown could restrain publication when this was clearly necessary in the public interest. However, he refused to grant an injunction to ban a book about events that had taken place a decade before. He found no grounds for saying that either the Crown or the individual civil servant had an enforceable right to have their advice treated as confidential for all time. Prompted by prosecuting counsel, he was prepared to say his remarks were about the Crossman case, thus enabling the government to claim the major issue of principle had been determined in their favour. After this setback, a committee of Privy Counsellors under Lord Radcliffe, set up to review the question of ministerial memoirs, concluded that a judge was not the best arbiter of the issue. Subsequently two further volumes of the Crossman diaries and the diaries of two other Labour Cabinet Ministers, Barbara Castle and Tony Benn, were published with no attempt at prior restraint.

The ABC Trial

The late 1970s produced an even more explosive mix of journalism and the OSA, when under the Labour Government of Jim Callaghan charges were brought against Aubrey, Berry and Campbell (hence the ABC trial) under section 1 as well as section 2. Crispin Aubrey and Duncan Campbell were young journalists who tape-recorded an interview with John Berry, a former army corporal, about his experiences in signals intelligence in Cyprus. They were arrested in February 1977 leaving Berry's flat. In 1976 the authorities had, it seems, wanted to prosecute Campbell in connection with an article *The Eavesdroppers* (about signals interception carried out by GCHQ and the US National Security Agency) written in collaboration with American journalist Mark Hosenball, who was subsequently deported. At the trial the prosecution set out to prove that Campbell's elaborate and extensive filing system on intelligence matters and communications was intended to be of use to an enemy 'for a purpose prejudicial to the safety and interests of the state' rather than the product of conscientious research for the purposes of investigative journalism. By producing a wealth of published material – including regimental magazines and the *Civil Service Yearbook* – the defence was repeatedly able to demonstrate that information claimed by prosecution witnesses to be highly secret was in fact publicly available, and after a strong hint from the judge the section 1 charges were eventually dropped. The defence contended that the OSA was to prevent harm to the nation's safety and not to save the government from embarrassment or to block newspaper investigations. The trial was a long drawn-out process. The first jury had to be discharged after it was revealed on television that jury vetting had taken place, and there was a re-trial in October 1978. By the end the proceedings had lasted a total of forty-two days at a cost of some £250,000. Before summing up, the judge took the unusual step of telling the defendants he had no intention of sending them to jail. The jury were out for nearly sixty-eight hours before finding all three defendants guilty of the section 2 charges. Berry was given a six-month suspended prison sentence and ordered to pay £250 in costs, while Aubrey and Campbell were both conditionally discharged and ordered to pay a proportion of the costs – under the original charges they could have gone to prison for thirty-two years. The outcome was widely seen as a victory for the defence, and a disaster for the government in that they had completely misjudged the case.

The Trial of Sarah Tisdall

In October 1983 the *Guardian* published details of government plans for dealing with the arrival of US cruise missiles at the RAF base at Greenham Common, a highly sensitive political issue at the time. The newspaper had received two documents, but it withheld one for security reasons and printed the document, classified secret, setting out the Defence Secretary's plans for handling parliamentary and public statements. The government went to court to force the *Guardian* to hand over the document, and this enabled the police to trace the source to a twenty-three year old clerk in the Foreign Secretary's private office. Sarah Tisdall confessed and was charged with a breach of section 2. At her trial in March 1984 she pleaded guilty, but afterwards defended her actions in a television programme, in which she spoke of the immorality of the Defence Secretary's deliberate attempt to avoid accountability in Parliament. The government's formal damage assessment only suggested that the disclosure might have involved some erosion of allied confidence in Britain as a partner to confidential exchanges. Mr Justice Cantley nevertheless sentenced her to six months' imprisonment, commenting on the need to make an example of the case and show that 'in these days' a plea that no harm had been done or even that disclosure was a good thing would not be a way of escaping a custodial sentence. The unexpected and disproportionate severity of the sentence provoked almost universal condemnation. The judge's attitude may also have encouraged the government to embark on the Ponting case a few months later.

The Trial of Clive Ponting

One of the most controversial episodes in the Falklands conflict was the sinking of the Argentinian cruiser *General Belgrano* by the British submarine *HMS Conqueror* on 2 May 1982, at a time when diplomatic efforts to negotiate a settlement were at a critical point. The version of events given to Parliament at the time by the Defence Secretary was untrue in several respects and gave the misleading impression that the *Belgrano* had been sailing towards, rather than away from, the British task force when it was torpedoed and sunk. In the course of persistent attempts, notably by Labour MP Tam Dalyell, to get at the facts, the Thatcher Government engaged in a prolonged cover-up. In July 1984 Clive Ponting, a senior civil servant in the Ministry of Defence, sent two documents to Dalyell that showed how he and the Foreign Affairs Select Committee were being misled. In August Ponting was charged with unauthorized disclosure under section 2. From the start the case attracted a great deal of publicity over the still politically sensitive *Belgrano* issue, the highly embarrassing question of whether the government had deliberately lied to Parliament, and the fact that it was the first prosecution under the OSA for giving information to a Member of Parliament. The ten-day trial in February 1985 provided the first full-scale airing of a public interest defence, with a former Home Secretary and a distinguished professor of English law and expert in the British constitution among those giving evidence for the defence. High level discussions within the MoD also received an unprecedented degree of exposure as the case progressed. Part of the trial was held in camera after the prosecution, which had admitted the documents sent to Dalyell contained unclassified information, had at a late stage introduced a top-secret intelligence document. In his summing up (described by one experienced observer as the most biased he had ever heard) Mr Justice McCowan dismissed the defence case almost out of hand and went on to rule that 'duty in the interest of the State' meant the same as official duty in the interests of the government of the day, and virtually directed the jury to convict. It took the jury just over an hour to bring in a unanimous verdict of not guilty. The result was widely seen as a political humiliation for the government and there was widespread criticism of the role of the Attorney-General, Sir Michael Havers, in what many people saw as a political prosecution brought by an embarrassed government.

The Case of Peter Wright: The Spycatcher Affair

The affair began in September 1985, when the Thatcher Government sought an injunction under the law of confidence in the Australian courts to prevent publication of *Spycatcher*, the memoirs of former MI5 officer, Peter Wright, who had settled in Tasmania after his retirement from the service in 1976. For many years Wright had been trying to expose his conviction that there had been a cover-up of the extent of continuing Soviet penetration of M15, and in particular of the fact that its former head, Sir Roger Hollis, had been a Soviet agent. Details of his thesis were already known through a dossier sent to the Prime Minister, two books by Chapman Pincher (*Their Trade is Treachery* and *Too Secret Too Long*) and Wright's own appearance in a Granada Television programme in 1984, yet the government was to justify its belated resort to legal action (later extended to Hong Kong and New Zealand) on the grounds that it must uphold the principle that members of the intelligence and security services have an absolute and lifelong duty to maintain confidentiality about their work. Publication of details of Wright's allegations by British newspapers also led the government to embark on an ultimately unsuccessful attempt to obtain a permanent injunction against any further publication. The immediate result of these legal moves was to arouse world-wide interest in *Spycatcher* and make it an international best-seller. In Britain public controversy focused on Wright's references to various illegal activities by MI5 and to a plot against the Wilson Government in 1974, but the government resisted the argument that the public interest or freedom of the press could override the requirement for confidentiality. In the Australian courts the prosecution's case, including the erratic previous record over publication of books about the intelligence services and the unforthcoming evidence of Cabinet Secretary Sir Robert Armstrong, did not hold up well. The defence denied any obligation of confidentiality because the material was either out of date or already publicly available, or exposed illegal acts, or had already been betrayed to the Soviet Union. This trial, like the other related legal actions and appeals at home and abroad lasting into 1988, ended in the failure of the government's case, an outcome again widely perceived as a humiliating and costly defeat, which had perversely ensured huge publicity for what might otherwise have been a relatively obscure and neglected book. The aftermath of the *Spycatcher* affair, with its exposure of illegal MI5 operations and of the risks of resort to the civil law of confidence, can be seen in two of the subsequent changes to the law introduced by Margaret Thatcher's Government: the Security Service Act (see chapter two) and certain provisions of the Official Secrets Act 1989 discussed in the final chapter.

6 Pressures for Change

Secrecy has rarely been high on the political agenda in Britain. This chapter is an account of the failure to reform the secrecy laws during the hundred years after the first Official Secrecy Act was passed in 1889. Despite a long history of criticism of section 2 of the 1911 Act, the most wide-ranging provision of them all, it remained in use for over seventy-five years. Since the 1960s other countries have introduced freedom of information laws, but Britain has opted instead for a new secrecy law, the fifth in the series.

The absence of vociferous popular demand for less secrecy reflects the fact that in a secretive country the extent of secrecy is itself a well-kept secret. This, together with a widespread mis-understanding about the real impact of the Official Secrets Act on everyday life, the mistaken assumption that it is all about spying, and the British tradition of deference and respect for authority, has contributed to the lack of sustained popular concern. But during the last twenty years there have nevertheless been periods when strong pressures for reform have built up, and politicians have felt the need to respond with promises to implement change. However, these pressures have not always been pushing in the same direction. While there has developed in recent years an increasingly vociferous and effective campaign urging liberalization of Britain's secrecy laws and pressing for positive measures to make government more open, others, less publicly, have wanted repeal of section 2 only to replace it with a readily enforceable law to act as an effective deterrent against leaks. It has also been a noticeable feature that parties in opposition have shown more enthusiasm for reducing government secrecy than parties in power.

Over the years there have been many ringing condemnations (from Sir Winston Churchill amongst others) of the iniquities of section 2 and its potential for abuse. These utterances were mostly sparked off by some particularly controversial use of the law. Not until the mid-1960s was there evidence of concerted pressure and signs of growing frustration with government secrecy. In 1965, following a controversy over the imprisonment of two journalists for refusing to reveal their sources for an article on a spy case, a joint working party of journalists and lawyers was set up on 'The Law and the Press' and the organization Justice produced a report containing proposals for reform of section 2, notably through inclusion of a public interest defence. This initiative provoked little more than a House of Lords' debate and a few unsuccessful private member's bills. Harder to ignore altogether was the criticism of excessive government secrecy made in the context of an official inquiry into the Civil Service. The 1968 Fulton Report found that public administration was surrounded by too much secrecy and recommended an inquiry to look at ways of getting rid of unnecessary secrecy. The Wilson Government's response was an internal inquiry with no outside consultation, leading to a White Paper in June 1969 entitled *Information and the Public Interest.* This argued that section 2 was not itself a barrier to greater openness and focused on the idea that the government should merely seek to widen the range of information it was prepared to release.

In 1970, the year of the controversial Aitken trial, a Conservative Government came to power with an election manifesto that included a promise to reduce unnecessary secrecy and review the OSA. Amid a storm of criticism of section 2, the Franks Committee was asked to review its operation. Their 1972 report recommended replacing section 1 of the OSA with an Espionage Act and section 2 with an Official Information Act that would restrict criminal sanctions to narrower and more specific categories of official information, and apply only to material classified secret or above. The Heath Government did no more than announce in 1973 that they accepted the essential recommendations of Franks, but needed more time to consider proposals.

`In its 1974 manifesto the Labour Party introduced a new element – the first hint of a move to freedom of information (FOI), reflecting an earlier internal study which had looked at the Swedish system of open government:

Labour believes that the process of government should be more open to the public. We shall: Replace the Official Secrets Act by a measure to put the burden on the public authorities to justify withholding information. (Ponting, 1985, p. 49)

68

In power Harold Wilson set up a new Cabinet committee (MISC 89), but there was little enthusiasm for introducing radical change. A visit to the United States by the Home Secretary Roy Jenkins convinced him that a British FOI Act would be costly, cumbersome and legalistic. The committee concentrated instead on proposals for reforming section 2, and amending action as well as unspecified liberalization were promised in the Queen's Speech of November 1975. After Harold Wilson resigned and James Callaghan took over as Prime Minister in April 1976 the climate changed. A massive inquiry into the leak of a highly embarrassing Cabinet document about plans to change child benefits did not lead to any prosecutions and Callaghan spoke of the need to make the OSA more effective. In November the new Home Secretary Merlyn Rees told MPs the government accepted the need for a new Official Information Act on the broad lines recommended by Franks and intended to change the OSA from a blunderbuss into an Armalite rifle (Hansard, 22 November 1976). Instead of any move towards freedom of information the Callaghan Government only held out the prospect of releasing more background material as a basis for better informed public debate and in early 1977 they used the existing OSA provisions to bring controversial charges against the press in the ABC case.

A new Cabinet committee (GEN 29) went ahead slowly with work on further categories of information to be protected under new legislation, and in July 1977 instructions were issued on implementing a new policy on disclosure (known as the 'Croham directive' after the then head of the Civil Service). The cautiously worded text was a confidential document, but its contents became public when leaked to *The Times*. It advised all permanent secretaries that 'the working assumption should be that all background material will be published' unless the responsible minister decided otherwise, but stressed that the initial step was to be 'modest' and should consist mainly of considering whether to make available 'deliberate presentations' prepared in the later stages of policy development (Ponting, 1985, pp. 53—7). There was a reminder of pressures to bring in measures on the lines of the US FOI Act and a warning that 'our prospects of being able to avoid such an expensive development here' might depend on results. A subsequent audit carried out in 1980 by *The Times* showed the directive had made very little difference to government output.

Growing dissatisfaction with the lack of official progress stimulated moves outsid Whitehall to press for more positive open government measures. At Westminster an All Party Committee on FOI was set up and in 1977 there was the first of a series of private member's bills on open government. A more moderate approach to reform, reflecting the traditional Whitehall approach, was advocated in a report produced by the Royal Institute for Public Administration. Its *Open Government: The British Interpretation,* although critical of government secrecy, felt openness would be better achieved through administrative discretion rather than legislation. The Royal Commission on the Press, which also reported in 1977, criticized the general level of secrecy in government, which it felt had caused much injustice, some corruption and many mistakes.

Although the Queen's Speech in November 1977 again promised legislative proposals to reform section 2, none were forthcoming. Outside pressure continued. In June 1978 Justice produced a report on FOI advocating a variant on the administrative approach, which would retain ministerial responsibility for decisions on release but provide for publication of guidelines and allow the parliamentary ombudsman to investigate complaints about ministerial failure to comply with the published guidelines. The following month the non-partisan Outer Circle Policy Unit presented their version of an FOI bill, which incorporated a statutory right of public access to government information outside certain specified categories. At Westminster the Conservative opposition arranged a debate on 15 June, in which they launched a savage attack on the failure to act. They condemned the government's inability to overcome 'the strenuous rearguard action mounted in the more obscurantist corners of Whitehall' (Hansard, 15 June 1978). The main attack on section 2 was mounted by the Shadow Attorney-General, Sir Michael Havers, who set out the case for substantial reform. In July 1978, four years after taking office, the Labour Government finally brought out a White Paper on reform of section 2. It claimed more official information was now being published, but contained no proposals for further moves, merely stating that the government had an open mind as to whether to move beyond 'a declared obligation, operating on a voluntary and discretionary basis' to a statutory duty of disclosure (Cmnd 7520).

This White Paper did little to reduce the mounting pressures for introducing some form of freedom of information as opposed to merely decriminalizing low-level leaks or promising more press releases. In October 1978 the National Executive Committee of the Labour Party produced its version of FOI. In February 1979 a report from the legal affairs committee of the Council of Europe invited member states which had not already done so to introduce a system of freedom of information.

In early 1979 the Callaghan Government was faced with the prospect of a private member's bill on FOI which was attracting considerable parliamentary support and seemed likely to be approved. Liberal MP Clement Freud had been well placed in the ballot and decided to introduce a bill to repeal section 2 and replace it with a right of access to official documents and a detailed schedule of specific exemptions. At the second reading in January 1979 Freud began by reminding the House of Commons that his proposals were consistent with Labour's declared policies for many years, and went on to make a scathing and witty attack on the absurdities of government secrecy. After wondering about what dark secrets of the White Fish Authority made it a taboo subject for parliamentary questions, he raised the effects of section 2:

> If one wants to find out how to look after one's children in a nuclear emergency, one cannot because it is an official secret; if one wants to know what noxious gases are being emitted from a factory chimney opposite one's house, one cannot because it is an official secret. A man who applies for a job as a gardener at Hampton Court was asked to sign form E74, in case he gave away information about watering begonias. What is worse, if someone is good enough to tell one, then one is an accessory to the crime. My contention is that Section 2 gives the Attorney-General more power than a bad man should have or a good man should need. (Hansard, 19 January 1979)

The government did not oppose the bill on second reading, but the Home Secretary warned that, although committed to greater openness in government, they were not giving 'a blank cheque'. The tactics they adopted were to introduce a great many amendments at the committee stage. Forced increasingly onto the defensive, they finally made clear their views on the legislative requirement and on freedom of information with a Green Paper, entitled *Open Government*, in March. This was accompanied by the findings of an inquiry by a team of officials from the Civil Service Department into practices elsewhere. After confirming their view that section 2 should be replaced by 'provisions that would restrict criminal sanctions for unauthorized disclosure to a strictly limited range of

71

information' and acknowledging that 'administration is still conducted in an atmosphere of secrecy that cannot always be justified', (Wilson, 1984, p. 131) the government came out firmly in favour of voluntary disclosure rather than right-to-know legislation as the correct course for Britain:

> The Government cannot accept that a statutory right of access which could affect adversely and fundamentally the accountability of Ministers to Parliament is the right course to follow. There are other methods of securing more open government which do not carry such damage ... A code of practice on access to official information, which the Government was fully committed to observe would be a major step forward. (Wilson, 1984, p. 131)

There were no specific proposals for such a code of practice, which in any case appeared to many as no more than a variant on the Croham directive and a recipe for carrying on much the same as before. Shortly afterwards the government fell, the Freud Bill was automatically lost and a Conservative Government under Margaret Thatcher was returned.

In the Queen's speech of May 1979 the new government said that: 'A measure will be introduced to replace the provisions of Section 2 of the Official Secrets Act with provisions appropriate to the present time'. As for policy on disclosing information, the Minister for the Civil Service indicated there would be no radical changes in this field:

> It will be the practice of this government to make such information as is possible available to the public including background papers and analytical studies relevant to major policy decisions. (Hooper, 1987, p. 232)

Monitoring of the Croham directive was abandoned – as an economy measure. In November a Protection of Official Information Bill was introduced. The Lord Chancellor described it as a code which was 'more liberal, more intelligible and even capable of enforcement'. There was to be no public right of access. The classes of protected information proposed by Franks had been modified; some were dropped but new ones were envisaged to cover the nationalized industries and all references to telephone tapping, mail interception and the work (or even the existence) of the intelligence agencies. It also included proposals for conclusive ministerial certificates (not challengeable in the courts) to be issued in respect of any alleged damage caused by unauthorized disclosures. The parliamentary debates happened to coincide with the revelation that the Russian spy named as 'Maurice' in Andrew Boyle's book *The Climate of Treason* was Anthony Blunt. When it became apparent that under this bill it would be illegal to discuss Blunt's identity the bill was dropped amid great controversy. The government made no move to introduce revised proposals. Despite the fact that the Lord Chancellor, Lord Hailsham, had described section 2 of the existing OSA as 'tolerable only because it is unenforceable and unenforced', (Hansard, 15 November 1979) the Attorney-General, Sir Michael Havers, went on to initiate a series of prosecutions under it.

Although freedom of information was now excluded altogether from the government agenda, the issue did not fade away. In 1981 Labour MP Frank Hooley introduced a new private member's bill but the government ensured its defeat at the second reading. At the 1983 general election both Labour and the Alliance parties promised to repeal section 2 and replace it with freedom of information legislation. In January 1984 a new Campaign for Freedom of Information was launched with the backing of many campaigning organizations and pressure groups which felt strongly that their work was seriously hampered by excessive government secrecy. The leaders of the three main opposition parties expressed their support for the campaign, but the Prime Minister's response was to reject the campaign's objectives as both inapppropriate and unnecessary under the British system:

> We already have a clear policy to make more information available and the necessary machinery to do so ... but above all ministers' accountability to Parliament would be reduced and Parliament itself diminished. (Wilson, 1984, pp. 134–5)

The counter-argument was put to MPs when in March David Steel, the Liberal leader, introduced his own Ten Minute Rule Bill on FOI: 'If ever there were a subject in which the collective will of Parliament should prevail over the government of the day, surely this is it' (Hansard, 6 March 1984). His move followed the outcry over the successful prosecution earlier that month of Sarah Tisdall and her sentence of six months' imprisonment on section

2 charges. The government made it clear that it was determined to prevent Civil Service leaks and to this end was fully prepared to continue using section 2. However, its use in the Ponting case proved still more controversial, and Ponting's unanimous acquittal in February 1985 effectively marked the end of that policy. Although the formal legal ruling (which held that the interests of the State were the same as the interests of the government of the day), a view subsequently endorsed by the Attorney-General, had the effect of foreclosing the option of a public interest defence, the verdict showed that a jury would not necessarily agree and could simply defy judicial guidance as to the law. This verdict, followed closely by the failure to bring any charges against Cathy Massiter after her revelations of unlawful activities by MI5, sparked off renewed demands among Conservative supporters for a more readily enforceable Act. However, in March 1985 a Home Office Minister made it clear there were no plans to bring in a public right of access or to reform section 2.

When in 1985 the government resorted to use of the civil law in an attempt to prevent publication of Peter Wright's book *Spycatcher*, this was widely seen as a substitute for its failure to use or reform the criminal law. The prolonged and ultimately unsuccessful use of the civil law of confidence did much to discredit the government's motives and its methods in pursuing Peter Wright and British newspapers through the courts at a time when, thanks to all the publicity generated, *Spycatcher* was a best-seller in many other countries. In the absence of any government moves to reform the secrecy laws, a Conservative backbencher, Richard Shepherd, decided to introduce his own proposals in November 1987. The Wright case had highlighted the question of whether 'prior publication' should be a legitimate defence, just as the Ponting case had focused public attention on the case for a 'public interest' defence. The Shepherd Bill provided for both of these. An unauthorized disclosure would have been justified if there were reasonable grounds to believe it revealed crime, fraud, abuse of authority, neglect in the performance of official duty or other misconduct and if the person concerned had taken reasonable steps to comply with any established procedure for drawing such misconduct to the attention of the appropriate authorities without effect. At the second reading in January 1988 the bill was lost by only thirty-seven votes, despite the use for the first time this century of a government three-line Whip to defeat a private member's bill.

In the face of outright government opposition to all such moves aimed at opening up central government the Campaign for Freedom of Information and its parliamentary supporters concentrated much of their efforts on introducing measures to reduce unnecessary secrecy in other areas of national life. Between 1985 and 1988 several private member's bills were successfully adopted. In 1985 Conservative MP Robin Squire's Local Government (Access to Information) Act extended rights of access to council meetings and related documentation. Similar access also applies to meetings and papers of Community Health Councils as a result of the Community Health Councils (Access to Information) Act 1988. As a result of Liberal MP Archy Kirkwood's Access to Personal Files Act 1987 council tenants have obtained the right to see their housing records, social services clients can see social work records, parents have access to their children's school records and students in local authority further education can see their own records. As from January 1989, under the Access to Medical Reports Act 1988, also introduced by Kirkwood, people have the right to inspect and amend records supplied by their doctor to insurance companies and employers. Labour MP Chris Smith has brought in the Environment and Safety Information Act 1988, which requires the regulating authorities to set up public registers of enforcement notices issued following a breach of safety and environmental laws. Although the pressures for a real reduction in official secrecy have failed to bring about change, in this way small but significant breaches have been made in the general culture of secrecy.

7 A New Secrecy Law

All democracies face the problem of reconciling the requirements of executive government with the demands of democratic control. Since the 1960s many other Western countries have introduced laws to make changes in what the government has a right to withhold and what the public has a right to know. Sweden's law on access to official documents dates from the eighteenth century, but more recently others have brought in reforming legislation of their own: the American Freedom of Information Act was passed in 1966 and strengthened in 1974; Norway and Denmark introduced their laws in 1970; France followed in 1978 and in the early eighties Canada, Australia and New Zealand all passed freedom of information acts. There are variations on the theme, but the basic thrust of such laws is to establish a legal right of access to government information, subject to certain exemptions, and introduce a right of appeal against a refusal by government to release information (by going to the courts or to a separate administrative tribunal or to an ombudsman). The areas most commonly granted exemption from public disclosure are defence, foreign affairs, national financial affairs and legal proceedings, with provisions aimed at protecting personal privacy and commercially sensitive information.

The extent to which these freedom of information acts do in fact provide more genuinely open government varies; for instance the Norwegian law allows the government to exempt whole classes of documents by decree, and Denmark's exceptions allow secrecy on the vague grounds that it is required by the 'special character of the circumstances'. But the fundamental change they all involve is the move from a situation where all information held by government is presumed to be secret unless it is decided otherwise to one where everything is presumed to be available unless it comes under one of the specifically exempted categories. In Britain, however, successive governments have taken the view that it is for the government itself to decide how open to be and what information may be released on any particular topic. This approach, so the argument goes, is an essential part of the Westminster system of government: the concept of ministerial responsibility to Parliament is not only incompatible with a statutory right of access but makes it unnecessary. In a letter to the Freedom of Information Campaign in 1984 Margaret Thatcher set out this view:

> Under our constitution Ministers are accountable to Parliament for the work of their Departments, and that includes the provision of information . . . A statutory right of access would remove this enormously important area of decision-making from Ministers and Parliament . . . (Wilson, 1984, p. 134–5)

This view has not prevailed in Australia, Canada and New Zealand, which all have Parliaments on the Westminster model and have introduced freedom of information. In Australia the Senate Standing Committee, which examined the case for and against freedom of information, acknowledged that the Westminster system could be used as a smokescreen to cover up existing practices of unnecessary secrecy. They found that far from being incompatible with it, a Freedom of Information Bill might in fact have the potential to strengthen the Westminster system by making the public service more open to public scrutiny and so more accountable for its actions. They were conscious of the threat to democracy posed by excessive government secrecy:

> The essence of democracy lies in the ability of the people to make choices: about who shall govern or about which policies they support or reject. Such choices cannot be made unless adequate information is available. It cannot be accepted that it is the government itself which has determined what level of information is to be regarded as adequate. (Australian Senate Standing Committee Report, 1979)

Reviewing the American experience of their freedom of information legislation in 1980, the US Attorney-General believed some important and positive changes had been brought about by less secrecy in the process of government. It had made federal government far more open, exposed government wrongdoing, made citizens better informed, and provided the data for an intelligent debate. In addition the Act had served to deter wrongful conduct by government officials because of fear of disclosure.

In April 1987, after the Zircon affair, the Thatcher Government began to consider what should replace section 2 of the Official Secrets Act, and in June 1988 Home Secretary Douglas Hurd produced a White Paper. It was concerned not with greater public access to information but only with the circumstances in which the unauthorized disclosure of official information should in future be a criminal offence. According to the White Paper, the proposals would allow for new legislation which would be 'easily comprehensible, readily applicable by the courts and widely accepted as useful and necessary'. In November 1988 a draft bill, consisting of 16 clauses, was presented to Parliament. It contained only relatively minor changes to the proposals contained in the White Paper.

The debate in the House of Commons took place in January and February 1989. Some of the bill's provisions, notably the lack of a public interest defence and the sweeping powers proposed in respect of intelligence information, were strongly criticized by senior Conservative backbenchers as well as by opposition MPs. To curtail debate and avoid the risk of amendment, the government took the unusual steps of taking the committee stage on the floor of the House and after only two days of debate introduced a guillotine motion.

The new legislation creates specific categories of information to be covered by criminal sanctions against unauthorized disclosure, and there are separate tests of likely harm for the different categories. In certain areas unauthorized disclosure will be an absolute offence − for example where any member or former member of the security and intelligence services (or non-members in certain designated posts) improperly discloses information, the prosecution will not need to produce any evidence of likely damage and the same applies to any information about interception of communications. In the other areas − defence, international relations and information useful to criminals − it will be for the prosecution to establish harm, but the definitions of what constitutes harm have been made much less strict than the test of 'serious injury' recommended by Franks. For instance, disclosure would only have to 'jeopardize the capability of the armed forces' and in the case of unauthorized disclosure of information passed in confidence from other governments or international organizations, the prosecution could claim the very fact of disclosure itself was damaging to Britain's international relations. The Act makes no provision for a public interest defence nor will prior publication in another country (except if made under their freedom of information legislation) be a defence.

The Official Secrets Act 1989 undoubtedly introduces one important and arguably long overdue change in the criminal law as it affects official information — many areas of government information will now be 'de-criminalized', that is no longer protected by the threat of a criminal prosecution in the event of unauthorized disclosure or receipt. Hence repeated claims by government ministers that this should be seen as a liberalizing measure. At the same time the Act introduces changes which will significantly strengthen the law in respect of information protected by criminal sanctions. It also introduces an entirely new offence of unauthorized publication. Whereas the 1911 Act applied primarily to Crown servants and created a separate offence of receipt of information, the new Act will make it an offence for *anyone* to disclose information in these categories without authorization and where they can reasonably be expected to know that harm is likely to be caused. There will be no need to show that a document has changed hands, as *publication* of information caught under the Act will be an offence. This means that tighter controls than ever before in peacetime have been imposed on the media. Moreover, the effect of the new Act is to remove or seriously restrict possible grounds for defence. It will no longer be possible for an official or a journalist to argue that a disclosure was justified because it revealed serious misconduct, corruption, fraud or negligence.

What effect, if any, is this new law likely to have on secrecy in Britain? When he was giving evidence to the Franks Committee, former Prime Minister James Callaghan said that in his view even if section 2 were reformed, things would go on much the same as before in government (Cmnd 5104, vol 4, p. 90). In the continued absence of moves to legislate for freedom of information or to guarantee the freedom of the press, this is likely to be the case. In presenting the bill to Parliament and the press, government ministers repeatedly described it as a liberalizing measure, but the emphasis in the government's own White Paper was on how to protect information: there was no mention of a move to greater openness. The document made it clear that other means of controlling information would continue. It pointed out that there may be circumstances where 'it is right for the Government to seek to enforce its rights on behalf of the public under the civil law of confidence, notwithstanding the fact that no prosecution for a criminal offence is possible (Cm 408, para. 14). In a section on the future role of the Civil Service discipline code, it stated:

> The result of implementing the government's proposals would be that only a very small proportion of the information in the hands of Crown servants would be protected by criminal law. That does not mean, however, that there will be no inhibition on the disclosure of any of the information which the criminal law will no longer protect . . . Once legislation is in place it will be necessary to amend the conduct rules for Crown servants, in particular the rule governing the disclosure of official information, to reflect the fact that the criminal law no longer protects all official information. (Cm 408, Paras 71 and 73)

This history of official secrecy ends as it began — with the introduction of secrecy legislation. In 1889 the first Official Secrets Act was passed. The fifth in the series, the Official Secrets Act of 1989, has now been adopted, marking the centenary of Britain's secrecy laws. When in the late nineteenth century the tightening of internal sanctions failed to prevent leaks, the government response was to introduce and strengthen criminal sanctions against unauthorized disclosure. Now that criminal sanctions no longer cover all government information, internal sanctions are to be tightened. There are other marked parallels with the past. Like the OSA of 1911, the new Act is a reaction to mounting frustration within government over the failure to deter leaks and many of its provisions are designed to avoid the embarrassment of unsuccessful prosecutions. In creating a new offence of unauthorized publication, this Act introduces for the first time powers that previous governments had wanted in order to control the press more effectively, but had hitherto failed to obtain. Opposition to the idea forced withdrawal of the 1908 Bill, and the 1911 Act confined itself to making receipt an offence. Whether the new Act will prove to be more comprehensible, more readily enforceable and more widely accepted than the old catch-all section 2 it replaces remains to be seen. It will depend on what cases the Attorney-General decides to bring, on how judges interpret concepts such as 'harm' and 'authorization' and on how public opinion and juries react.

Official Secrets Acts are not the cause of secrecy, only its symptoms. When the Franks Committee looked at the operation of section 2 and its effects on government, they felt that factors such as constitutional arrangements, political traditions, national character and habits and ways of thought all had a major influence on the extent of openness in government. Britain's long standing culture of secrecy and tradition of closed government will not disappear with the repeal and replacement of section 2. The 1989 Official Secrets Act merely alters the way information is controlled; it allows no more disclosure of information than before. The Act itself does nothing to reduce official secrecy in Britain.

Bibliography and References

General

Andrew, Christopher 1985: *Secret Service: Making of the British Intelligence Community.* London: Heinemann.

Andrew, Christopher and Dilks, David (eds) 1984: *The Missing Dimension: Governments and Intelligence Communities in the Twentieth Century.* London: Macmillan.

Birkinshaw, Patrick 1988: *Freedom of Information: The Law,the Practice and the Ideal.* London: Weidenfeld and Nicolson.

Campbell, Duncan 1981: *Big Brother is Listening: Phonetappers and the Security State,* New Statesman Report, 2. London: New Statesman.

Campbell, Duncan 1983: *War Plan UK: The Secret Truth about Britain's Civil Defence.* London: Paladin.

Cockerell, Michael, Hennessy, Peter and Walker, David 1984: *Sources Close to the Prime Minister.* London: Macmillan.

Crossman, Richard 1975–7: *Diaries of a Cabinet Minister.* 3 vols. London: Hamish Hamilton and Jonathan Cape.

Delbridge, Rosemary and Smith, Martin (eds) 1982: *Consuming Secrets: How Official Secrecy affects Everyday Life in Britain.* London: Burnett Books.

Hooper, David 1987: *Official Secrets: The Use and Abuse of the Act.* London: Secker and Warburg.

Leigh, David 1980: *The Frontiers of Secrecy.* London: Junction Books.

May, Annabelle and Rowan, Kathryn (eds) 1982: *Inside Information: British Government and the Media.* London: Constable.

Michael, James 1982: *The Politics of Secrecy: Confidential Government and the Right to Know.* Harmondsworth: Penguin.

Palmer, Alasdair 1984: The History of the D-Notice Committee, in Andrew and Dilks (eds), 1984.

Ponting, Clive 1985: *The Right to Know.* London: Sphere.

Ponting, Clive 1986: *Whitehall: Tragedy and Farce.* London: Hamish Hamilton.

Robertson, K.G. 1982: *Public Secrets: A study in the Development of Government Secrecy.* London: Macmillan.

Stuart, C. 1975: *The Reith Diaries.* London: Cassell

Williams, David 1965: *Not in the Public Interest.* London: Hutchinson.

Wilson, Des 1984: *The Secrets File.* London: Heinemann Educational.

Wilson, Harold 1975: *The Governance of Britain.* London: Weidenfeld and Nicolson

Young, Hugo 1976: *The Crossman Affair.* London: Hamish Hamilton and Jonathan Cape.

Official Publications

Command Papers

Cmd 9163 *Report of the Committee on Departmental Records* (Grigg Report), 1954.

Cmnd 283 *Report of the Committee on the Interception of Communications* (Birkett Report), 1967.

Cmnd 3309 *Report on D-Notice Matters* (Radcliffe Report), 1967.

Cmnd 3638 *The Civil Service* (Fulton Report), 1968.

Cmnd 4089 *Information and the Public Interest* (White Paper), 1969.

Cmnd 5104 *Report and Evidence of the Committee on Section 2 of the Official Secrets Act 1911* (Franks Report), 1972.

Cmnd 6386 *Report on Ministerial Memoirs* (Radcliffe Report), 1976.

Cmnd 7520 *Open Government* (Green Paper), 1979.

Cmnd 8787 *Falklands Islands Review: Report of the Committee of Privy Councillors* (Franks Report), 1983.

Cm 408 *Reform of Section 2 of the Official Secrets Act 1911*, 1988.

Other publications

Disclosure of Information: A Report on Overseas Practice. Civil Service Department, 1979.

Senate Standing Committee on Constitution and Legal Affairs: *Freedom of Information.* Australian Government Publishing Service, 1979.

Index

84